Aerial photographs of lower Broadway and the Newburgh riverfront show the corporate headquarters building of Key Bank as it nears completion. Courtesy of Key Bank

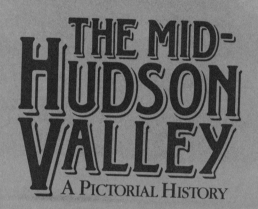

THE MID-HUDSON VALLEY

A PICTORIAL HISTORY

ROBERT PAUL MOLAY

Robert Paul Molay

A limited edition of 4,000
copies, of which this is number _1,346_

KEY BANK

THE MID-HUDSON VALLEY

A Pictorial History

Robert Paul Molay

Designed by Sharon Varner Moyer

THE
DONNING COMPANY
PUBLISHERS
NORFOLK/VIRGINIA BEACH

To:
Joy
The sweetest chapter
in my personal history

Copyright © 1987 by Robert Paul Molay

The Donning Company/Publishers
5659 Virginia Beach Boulevard
Norfolk, Virginia 23502

Edited by Nancy O. Phillips

Library of Congress Cataloging-in-Publication Data

Molay, Robert Paul, 1941-
    The Mid-Hudson Valley.

    Bibliography: p.
    Includes index.
    1. Hudson River Valley (N.Y. and N.J.) —History—
Pictorial works. 2. Hudson River Valley (N.Y.
and N.J.)—Description and travel—Views. I. Title.
F127.H8M65   1987   974.7'3'0222   87-24522
ISBN 0-89865-606-0 (lim. ed.)

Printed in the United States of America

Table of Contents

Foreword

Ever since the first decade of the 1600s, when Henry Hudson sailed the *Half Moon* up our river, the Mid-Hudson Valley has played a vital role in the development of the American Republic. The relatively short stretch of the Hudson River that passes through Newburgh, Poughkeepsie, and Kingston was particularly important in the earliest days of Dutch settlement, the English colonial period, and the Revolutionary War.

Newburgh, Poughkeepsie, and Kingston grew to greatness in the nineteenth century as river cities. First there were the wind-powered sloops and whaling vessels, then the great sidewheeling steamers bringing bustling activity and prosperity in their wake.

The river cities in the Mid-Hudson Valley experienced a sad period of decline in this century when technology advanced, patterns of transportation changed, and the mighty Hudson River became less important to the economy of this region and the nation. Architectural-landmark buildings became unused, neglected eyesores. Priceless riverfront properties stood vacant for decades.

This pattern of decline has now been definitively reversed. Productive new uses are being found for the treasures of the past. The beauty of the river, the relative mildness of the climate, the glory of the changing seasons, the uncrowded quality of life available here, the easy access to New York City—all these assets are bringing renewed vigor to Newburgh, Poughkeepsie and Kingston.

It has been my pleasure and honor to serve as the chief executive of Orange County government over the past ten years. The place, the river, the people who live here, the history and cultural richness we have, taken together contributes to the great bounty we know as the Hudson River Valley.

Robert Paul Molay is at his creative best in this fine book. Mr. Molay's pictorial history comes at a particularly appropriate time in the evolution of the Mid-Hudson Valley, when an appreciation of our past will help us to meet the responsibilities of the future.

—Louis Heimbach
County Executive
Orange County, N.Y.

Acknowledgments

From the moment this project was conceived and its broad outlines were planned, it benefited at every stage from the suggestions, assistance, and—above all—encouragement of Thomas Kyle, executive director of the Historical Society of Newburgh Bay and Highlands. It is fair to say that this book could not have been completed without Mr. Kyle's expert assistance. However, any errors or omissions are solely the fault of the author.

Alfred P. Marquart of Kingston generously opened his home to a stranger, placing at my disposal his valuable collection of rare old books and pictures. Mr. Marquart is a true *amateur* in the original sense of the word, an accomplished scholar of Hudson River lore who is motivated by a deep love for his chosen subject matter.

Other important contributors to this effort include Mrs. Valice Ruge, Old Prints of the Hudson; Edwin M. Ford, historian of the city of Kingston; William Vacca, Key Bank; Helen VerNooy Gearn, historian of the city of Newburgh; Robert Eurich, Hill-Hold Museum; Joy Virginia O'Flaherty, collector of Indian artifacts; Oliver Shipp, historian of the town of Newburgh; and Margery Shipp.

Valued suggestions were also gratefully received from Michael Brown, the William Bull and Sarah Wells Family Association, Inc.; Constitution Island Association, West Point; Brendan O. Coyne, director of public information, Mount Saint Mary College, Newburgh; Donald C. Gordon, historian of the town of New Windsor; Jean Guinup, Brotherhood Winery, Washingtonville; J. Dolly Kohler, Newburgh; Nan Sleight, Marlboro; and William Stone, Highland Falls.

Reaching far back in time to the paleo-Indian culture of eastern New York State, this projectile found near Bloomingburg has been identified as a Lamoka point, of the type made between 3500 and 2500 B.C. Photograph by Robert Paul Molay, courtesy Joy V. O'Flaherty

CHAPTER 1

The Hudson Before Henry Hudson

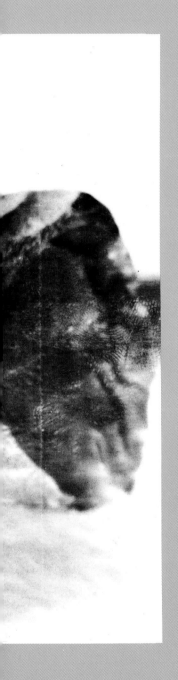

The Hudson is salty.

The portion that flows through the old New York State communities of Newburgh, Poughkeepsie and Kingston is technically considered an estuary, or arm of the Atlantic Ocean, rather than a true river. Like the rest of the ocean, the 151-mile stretch from Troy to New York harbor is subject to the ebb and flow of tides, and once supported abundant marine life.

For many centuries before the arrival of Henry Hudson in 1609, the area now known as the Mid-Hudson Valley was home to various branches of the Algonquin people. Their ancestral legends spoke of the water-that-flows-two-ways—a simple, yet eloquent description of the estuary phenomenon.

On the west bank of the river, extending west-ward to the Delaware River, were tribes belonging to the Lenape alliance of the Algonquins. In the vicinity of Newburgh the Quassaick Indians gave their name to the first European settlement. Further north, around Kingston, were the Esopus or Waynawanck Indians.

Another branch of the Algonquins inhabited the east bank of the river. These were the Wappingi people, whose name is preserved today in Wappingers Falls and Wappingers Creek.

It is a bewildering task—far beyond the scope of this pictorial history—to attempt to sort out all the variant spellings and alternate names of peoples and places from the early days of European visitation and settlement in the Mid-Hudson Valley. The people we call the Indians had no written alphabet, and their words would have fallen differently on the ears of the Dutch, English, and French chroniclers who tried to write down the sounds they heard.

Some of these tribes were apparently quite small, living in narrowly defined territories. The Matteawans inhabited the vicinity of Beacon, on the opposite side of the river from Newburgh, and it was the Waoranecks who performed the ritual Kintikaye on the flat rock in the river north of Newburgh that the Dutch called the Devil's Dance Chamber.

According to Edmund Platt, the historian of record for Poughkeepsie, the name was originally *Uppuqui-lpis-lng*, a "spring with a waterfall" within the current city limits. A transitional spelling was Pooghkepesingh. The Indian clearing where Kingston stands today was called Atkarkarton by the Esopus tribe.

The water-that-flows-two-ways has had many names. Before Hudson's arrival in September 1609 it was known as the Mannahatta or the Shatemuc. Henry Hudson referred to it as the Great River of the Mountains. During the days when it was under the control of the Dutch West India Company it was renamed the River of the Prince Mauritius, to honor Maurice of Orange. The British took over from the Dutch on September 8, 1664, and it became Hudson's River.

Even during the days of Dutch rule the Hudson had also been called the North River. Robert Fulton's pioneering vessel, which made its first commercial run from New York City to Albany on September 4, 1807, was never called the *Clermont*—Fulton registered her as the *North River Steam Boat*.

Before the advent of Europeans in the Mid-Hudson Valley, the local tribes had some objects made of copper, but apparently none of these objects were their tools or weapons. They chipped and flaked projectile points from local flint and other suitable materials, as their ancestors had done for eons. These mementos of our Stone Age heritage continue to turn up in the Mid-Hudson region, particularly in favorably situated cornfields at spring plowing time.

The age-old cultural patterns were disrupted permanently when the early settlers sold two commodities to the Indians—guns and rum. The rest, as they say, is history.

A projectile point from Narrowsburg evokes memories of the ancient Lenape and Minsi peoples who occupied this Delaware River country and played such an important role in the early histories of Orange and Ulster counties. Photograph by Robert Paul Molay, courtesy of Joy V. O'Flaherty

Percussion chipping on the shiny black eastern New York State flint identifies this spearpoint as the Snook Kill type, widely distributed throughout the Hudson River Valley below Albany. This specimen found in Campbell Hall, central Orange County. Photograph by Robert Paul Molay, courtesy of Joy V. O'Flaherty

Another projectile point found in Campbell Hall was also chipped from New York State flint by the former inhabitants of the Mid-Hudson Valley. Photograph by Robert Paul Molay, courtesy of Joy V. O'Flaherty

7

A Hudson River steamboat with twin smoke-stacks (center, right) is already challenging the supremacy of sailing vessels in this nine-teenth-century engraving by W. M. Bartlett and R. Wallis, showing the view from the Siege Battery—now known as Trophy Point—at West Point. Looking upriver, the entrance is seen to Newburgh Bay and the Hudson Highlands. At right (the east bank) are Constitution Island, Mount Taurus and Break Neck; at left are Cro'Nest and the Storm King, with Pollopell's (Bannerman's) Island dimly visible in the distance. Courtesy of Alfred P. Marquart

CHAPTER 2

Days and Nights of River Travel

When I walked down to the foot of West Forty-first Street in New York City on a balmy summer Saturday in 1967, to buy a steamship excursion ticket, I had no background knowledge to help me understand the glorious tradition of the Hudson River Day Line.

Like thousands of my fellow passengers, I got off at Bear Mountain State Park. The steamer continued chugging its way upriver to the Poughkeepsie Railroad Bridge, where it wheeled about for the return trip. Frolicking in the public swimming pool at Bear Mountain had left me pleasantly exhausted, and I was glad when my steamer returned to carry me home. I remember that the price of passage seemed surprisingly reasonable, that the ship itself was immaculate, and that the crowd on board was friendly but certainly not rowdy. Beyond these observations, I was aware of nothing remarkable about my excursion on the Hudson River.

I know now that the steamer was the *Alexander Hamilton*, last in the proud succession of elegant ships that had been operated by the Day Line since 1863. That tradition endured for only a few more years, ending with the final trip of the *Alexander Hamilton* in 1972.

Today, sadly, the Hudson River is no longer a practical artery for passenger travel between New York City and Albany. In the era of regularly scheduled steamer service, there really was a sense of community extending from Newburgh to Poughkeepsie to Kingston, in the region that is the focus of this pictorial history.

For two hundred years after Henry Hudson's visit, sailing sloops not unlike the *Half Moon* carried on vigorous trade along the entire tidewater portion of the Hudson River. Then Robert Fulton demonstrated the practicality of steam propulsion in 1807.

Although steamboats eventually dominated the river traffic, sailing craft never totally disappeared. New England whaling vessels docked for a time at

Newburgh—long enough to give rise to the quaint expression, "Greasy luck!" This was the farewell wish called out at the Newburgh dock by families of departing crewmen on the whalers, referring to the blubber from which the precious illuminating oil was extracted.

Until recent decades, the Hudson River froze solid in the winter. On the riverbanks in the Mid-Hudson region enormous ice houses were clustered for storing this commodity until the warm season. The Day Line steamers generally ceased service from October through May, meaning that alternative modes of transportation were needed even in the greatest days of river travel. The region's excellent network of railroads, highways, and even regional airports combined to render the steamer service unprofitable.

JUST LANDED,

From on board Sloops *Union & Magdalen*,
74 hhds. 3d and 4th proof
ST. CROIX RUM,
18 ditto 4th and 5th JAMAICA do.
6 Casks PORT,
9 do. RED, } WINES.
6 qr casks MALAGA, } WINES.
5 butts COGNLAC BRANDY,
6 pipes GIN,
With a very general supply of
GROCERIES, to be sold by
James and Archibald Kane.
Albany 19th May, 1801.

A rare, poorly preserved old photograph shows three sailing vessels tied up along Newburgh's Water Street, with some familiar landmarks barely visible in the distance. The building second from the left is the Newburgh Plaster Works. Courtesy of the Historical Society of Newburgh Bay and the Highlands

From the earliest days of European settlement in the Mid-Hudson Valley, the river was an important artery of trade. A newspaper advertisement in the collection of the Historical Society of Newburgh Bay and the Highlands attracted the attention of readers to a shipment of alcoholic beverages brought to Albany by sloop in 1801. Courtesy of Helen VerNooy Gearn

A replica of Robert Fulton's original North River Steam Boat *was planned, after painstaking research, by Frank E. Kirby and J. W. Millard. Misnamed the* Clermont, *it shared top billing in the Hudson-Fulton Celebration of 1909, along with a replica of Henry Hudson's* Half Moon, *donated by the Dutch government. This photograph shows the* Clermont *being towed from Newburgh to Poughkeepsie by the* Norwich, *built in 1836*

and surely at that time the oldest steamer in the world still in service. The Hudson River Day Line purchased the Clermont *and stationed her at Poughkeepsie as a floating museum from May 24, 1911, through the fall of 1914. The* Clermont *spent her last days in a tidal lagoon off Kingston Point, and was finally broken up in 1939. Courtesy of Key Bank*

Sailing ships brought the first Europeans to the Hudson River Valley and, even after Robert Fulton's "teapot" had demonstrated the practicality of steam travel on the river, tall-masted sloops continued to play an important role in the region's economic life. The advertisement for a freight line that ran between Saugerties and New York City is from a Kingston newspaper in 1829. Courtesy of the Historical Society of Newburgh Bay and the Highlands

Clermont *was the name of the home of New York State Chancellor Robert Livingston, who bankrolled Robert Fulton in the development of the first practical Hudson River steamboat, named the* North River Steam Boat *when she was enrolled for service on September 3, 1807. Fulton's first biographer, Cadwallader D. Colden, appears to have been responsible for misnaming this pioneer steamer the* Clermont, *an error that has since been transmitted to untold millions. Courtesy of Alfred P. Marquart*

Best loved of all the Hudson River steamers was the Mary Powell. *She was built in Jersey City in 1861, with a wooden hull 267 feet long, two boilers and a vertical beam engine to power her massive side-wheel. Courtesy of Alfred P. Marquart*

The cover of a timetable for the Mary Powell *indicates that it is from the 1885-1913 era, when A. Eltinge Anderson was her skipper. He was the son of the original owner and captain, Absalom L. Anderson. From the collection of Robert Paul Molay*

When time permitted, the passenger on the Mary Powell could luxuriate in a round trip to New York City entirely by Hudson River steamer. The timetable also offered an array of alternatives for cutting short the trip by linking up to one of the Hudson Valley's railroad lines, or making connections to other destinations by ferry or stage. From the collection of Robert Paul Molay

The Mary Powell's distinguished career on the Hudson River lasted from 1861 to 1917. It was only from 1903 to the end of her service that she was part of the Hudson River Day Line. Her home port was Rondout (Kingston). Although the Mary Powell was never actually raced, she was widely reputed to be the fastest passenger ship on the river. Courtesy of Alfred P. Marquart

Frank Leslie's Illustrated Newspaper *focused national attention on the winter sport of ice boating, as practiced in the Mid-Hudson Valley. An engraving from the edition of February 8, 1879, shows a curious passenger mix of a flock of sheep sharing the ride with a pair of fashionably dressed ladies. Courtesy of the Historical Society of Newburgh Bay and the Highlands*

Another scene from the same edition of Frank Leslie's Illustrated Newspaper *shows what appears to be Storm King Mountain, in the Hudson Highlands, in the background of an action-packed ice-boating tableau. Courtesy of the Historical Society of Newburgh Bay and the Highlands*

A watercolor by the American artist Reynolds Beal, dated 1884, shows many types of river craft, including a jaunty tugboat. In the lower right is the West Shore Railroad, in a view looking southward into the highlands of the Hudson River. Courtesy of Valice Ruge, Old Prints of the Hudson

In an era when many aspects of American culture had their rough edges, steamboat travel on the Hudson River proudly maintained a genteel family atmosphere. The Hudson River Day Line, in particular, fought off economic pressures to sell alcoholic drinks and operate on Sundays. This cheerful group of passengers of all ages, aboard the Mary Powell, is taking fullest advantage of the wholesome air and inspiring scenery in the Hudson Highlands. Courtesy of Alfred P. Marquart

Toward the end of her years on the Hudson River, the Mary Powell *was used for excursions between New York City and Bear Mountain, for charter service, and for carrying passengers from Kingston, Poughkeepsie, and Newburgh to hear evangelist Billy Sunday preach in New York City. She made her last trip on September 5, 1917. Courtesy of Alfred P. Marquart*

Central-Hudson Steamboat Company was organized in 1899, consolidating three former operators of Hudson River night lines. Poughkeepsie Transportation Company ran between Poughkeepsie and New York City; Homer Ramsdell Transportation Company ran between Newburgh and New York; and Romer & Tremper Steamboat Company ran between Kingston and New York. Unlike the side-wheeling day steamers, the Homer Ramsdell *was driven by propeller. During the hard years of the Depression, in 1930, she was sold for use as an excursion boat in Massachusetts and renamed the* Allerton. *Courtesy of Helen VerNooy Gearn*

The Mary Powell *was based in Rondout and always stopped there, except for four experimental trips to Albany in 1872. But the Hudson River Day Line's through steamers to Albany, for most of the nineteenth-century, saved precious time by picking up and discharging Kingston passengers on the east side of the river at Rhinecliff (always called Rhinebeck by the Day Line announcer). The ferryboat* Transport, *shown in this postcard view, was part of the service that provided communication between the east and west banks. After 1896, with the development of a suitable landing at Kingston Point Park, the Day Line through steamers stopped at Kingston rather than Rhinebeck. Courtesy of Alfred P. Marquart*

Not every voyage by Hudson River steamer ended happily. This photograph shows the sinking of the Emeline. *Courtesy of the Historical Society of Newburgh Bay and the Highlands*

Another shipwreck on the Hudson, probably at Kingston, is shown in this photograph. Courtesy of Alfred P. Marquart

17

The river steamer at center, the C. W. Morse, *was put into service in 1904 by the People's Line, a quondam competitor of the Hudson River Day Line. Her owners claimed that she cost $1 million. The ship was named for Charles Wyman Morse, the multimillionaire "Ice King" who began plotting to acquire the Day Line in 1902. Courtesy of the Historical Society of Newburgh Bay and the Highlands*

This scene was photographed at the Hudson-Fulton Celebration of 1909. Courtesy of the Historical Society of Newburgh Bay and the Highlands

Newburgh

Newburgh's first European settlers were Germans from a principality called Newburgh in the Palatinate, or Rhineland region of the former Holy Roman Empire.

Conditions of life had become unbearably hard in the Palatinate as the result of three factors: the invasion in 1707 by the French army under Marshall Villars, taxes that reduced the residents to starvation, and an unprecedented cold winter in 1708 that killed the region's fruit trees and grape vines.

On the first trip a group of forty-one Rhinelanders left to settle along the Hudson River at Quassaick Creek, with the permission and assistance of Queen Anne's British government. The religious makeup of this group was fifteen Lutherans and twenty-six Calvinists.

Although they undoubtedly found religious freedom in their new-world settlement, the Rhinelanders found life harsh and survival difficult. The Palatine Patent was granted by the Queen in 1719, but the nine original landholders soon afterward decided to pull up stakes and resettle elsewhere. Many went to the vicinity of Lancaster, Pennsylvania, which is today known as Pennsylvania Dutch country.

The owners sold the Palatine Patent in 1752. One of the purchasers was Alexander Colden, who had received the queen's authorization to establish the Newburgh-Fishkill ferry service in 1743.

The original settlement, on a sheltered bay of the Hudson near the mouth of the Quassaick Creek, was about two miles south of the present-day city of Newburgh. When New York State was organized into towns in 1788, this site became part of the town of New Windsor.

Entering Newburgh today on the main north-south highway that parallels the Hudson, one sees welcoming signs that characterize Newburgh as the "Birthplace of the Republic." While this claim might raise a few eyebrows in Philadelphia, Boston, Lexington, Concord, and even in New York City, the

Lewis Moses Gomez, identified in many sources as Gomez the Jew, was an early associate in the fur trade with John Jacob Astor. Gomez built this water-powered mill in 1714 to grind flour. In the early 1920s it was reconstructed by Dard Hunter, an authority on papermaking, but an inadequate flow of water prevented the mill from producing the fine-textured paper Hunter had envisioned. Long unused, and now administered by a foundation, the old mill has deteriorated considerably since this view was taken in 1981. Both the mill and the house that Gomez built and occupied are on Mill House Road, straddling the border between the towns of Marlborough and Newburgh. Photograph by Robert Paul Molay

associations with George Washington are particularly strong and meaningful here. By comparison to the hundreds of hotels throughout the Eastern Seaboard that advertise "Washington Slept Here," Washington actually set up long-term housekeeping in Newburgh—long enough to bring Martha into the picture—in 1782-1783.

The beautiful stone house known today as Washington's Headquarters was built in 1750 by Jonathan Hasbrouck, who had also built Orange County's first gristmill on the Quassaick or Chambers Creek. The Hasbrouck House is approached on the west side from Liberty Street, in a section of Newburgh known affectionately as Washington Heights. As Liberty Street is one of the longer arteries of the city and passes through neighborhoods of varying character, residents of the Heights take special pains to include the "W. H." as part of their street addresses.

There are no Revolutionary War battles associated with Newburgh. After the Continental victory over Lord Cornwallis at Yorktown, the triumphant army was brought from Virginia to the New Windsor Cantonment to await the negotiation of a formal cessation of hostilities with the British. Washington's army had not been paid and, during that long final winter encampment in the vicinity of Temple Hall, there were stirrings of mutiny.

In desperation, some of Washington's most trusted officers sent him a letter offering to scrap the idea of a democratic form of government and to crown Washington as king. Washington spurned this offer in forceful language and it is perhaps from this event that Newburgh can claim with some justice to be the birthplace of the republic.

Before the great days of railroad building, until the 1840s, Newburgh grew rapidly as the result of vigorous river commerce. But the New York & Erie Railroad originally bypassed Newburgh to stop in Goshen, instead. The Erie was later required to build a branch to Newburgh, largely due to the effective lobbying of shipping magnate Homer Ramsdell.

In the 1950s, Newburgh seemed to embody every American's ideal of the perfect small city. It had beautiful, scenic surroundings, lovingly tended parks, and jobs for everyone who wanted to work in a balanced variety of industries. The ferry to Beacon, the dependable river steamers, and the railroads on the west bank of the river all combined to make Newburgh's Water Street into one of the Hudson Valley's greatest shopping districts.

For about the next two decades, Newburgh went through a painful reassessment of its assets. There was no longer passenger service on the rails, the river, or the ferry. Shoppers were showing preference for the new style of suburban malls. Long-established industries were discovering the advantages of the Sun Belt and skipping town. The policies of urban renewal, practiced on a nationwide scale, favored demolishing some unused structures that could have been left standing until new uses were found.

By 1980, Newburgh was ready for a revival. It was spearheaded by Mayor Joan M. Shapiro, who almost single-handedly created the psychological climate for renewed faith and investment in her beloved city. Many others diligently negotiated the details of each deal and provided the necessary administrative support, but it was "Joanie's" boundless energy and persuasive salesmanship that must be credited for actually getting the shovels breaking ground and the wheels of industry and commerce turning once again in Newburgh.

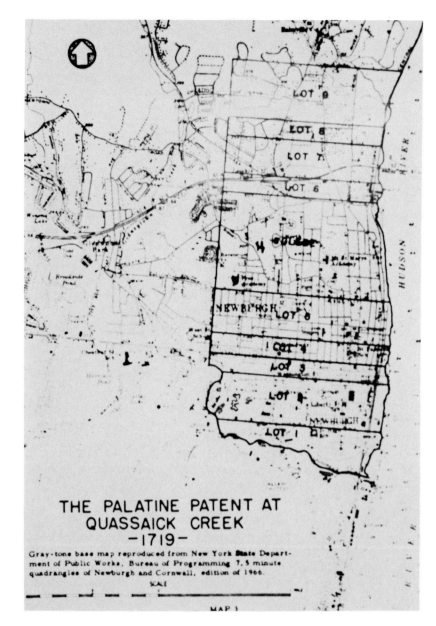

THE PALATINE PATENT AT
QUASSAICK CREEK
—1719—

Gray-tone base map reproduced from New York State Department of Public Works, Bureau of Programming 7.5 minute quadrangles of Newburgh and Cornwall, edition of 1966.

SCALE

MAP 3

The Palatine Patent was granted by Queen Anne to the first European settlers who came to Newburgh in 1709. They were Germans, from a principality called Newburgh in the Palatinate, or Rhineland region, of the former Holy Roman Empire. The Palatines had first fled to England from their homeland to escape religious persecution. They settled among the Quassaick Indians at the Quassaick (otherwise known as Chambers') Creek. Many later moved to Pennsylvania, where they became known as the Pennsylvania Dutch. Courtesy of the Historical Society of Newburgh Bay and the Highlands

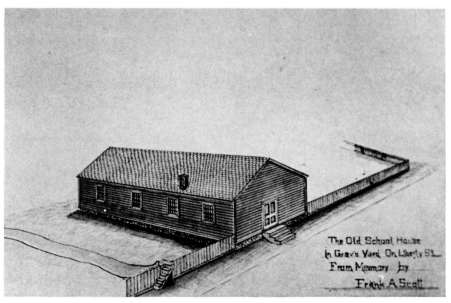

The Old School House in Grave Yard On Liberty St. From Memory by Frank A Scott

Memories of early settlement in Newburgh are evoked in this reconstruction of the old school house in the graveyard on Liberty Street, drawn from memory by Frank A. Scott. Courtesy of the Historical Society of Newburgh Bay and the Highlands

Another artistic effort to preserve the past by Frank A. Scott is this drawing of the first Methodist Episcopal Church at the intersection of Gidney Avenue and Liberty Street. Courtesy of the Historical Society of Newburgh Bay and the Highlands

First M.E. Church
Corner Of Gidney Avenue & Liberty Street
From Memory by Frank A. Scott

This photograph, labeled "Mrs. Miller's Tobacco Factory, Moodna, New Windsor, New York," shows an ancient stone building at a site that had been occupied by mills of various types since the very early days of European settlement around Newburgh. Courtesy of the Historical Society of Newburgh Bay and the Highlands

Cadwallader Colden, a resident of Ulster County, served as lieutenant governor of the colony of New York from 1760 until after the Battle of Lexington in 1775. He was also acting governor for part of this period. His portrait was painted by John Wollaston, active from 1751 through 1769, and bequeathed by Grace Wilks to the Metropolitan Museum of Art in 1922. Courtesy of the Historical Society of Newburgh Bay and the Highlands

Another Cadwallader Colden, distinguished from his earlier namesake as Cadwallader D. Colden, of Coldenham in the town of Newburgh, lived from 1769 to 1834. He was a mayor of New York City, a state senator, a congressman, a scientist and philosopher, a friend of Chancellor Robert Livingston, and the biographer of Robert Fulton. There is a monument to his memory in St. George's Church at Tenth Street and Broadway in New York City. Courtesy of the Historical Society of Newburgh Bay and the Highlands

The wife of Cadwallader Colden, Mrs. Alice Christie Colden, was also painted by John Wollaston. Courtesy of the Historical Society of Newburgh Bay and the Highlands

This photograph of C. A. Colden of 28 Colden Street was taken by W. W. Whiddit, 88 Water Street, Newburgh. Her relationship to the rest of the Colden family is unknown. Courtesy of the Historical Society of Newburgh Bay and the Highlands

25

An unusual perspective on Washington's Headquarters on Liberty Street, the Hasbrouck House built in 1750, distinguishes this painting done in 1830 by Raphael Hoyle. Courtesy of the Historical Society of Newburgh Bay and the Highlands

A drawing by R. A. Weed shows the main exterior architectural features of Washington's Headquarters. Courtesy of the Historical Society of Newburgh Bay and the Highlands

An informal drawing dated 1918 and signed by "Mahonri Young" shows the citizens of Newburgh relaxing in the park surrounding the Washington's Headquarters historic site—much as they do today. Courtesy of the Historical Society of Newburgh Bay and the Highlands

The east facade of the Hasbrouck House was photographed by William Henry Mapes, who was active in Newburgh around the turn of the century. Courtesy of the Historical Society of Newburgh Bay and the Highlands

The room with seven doors and one window, a well-known peculiarity of Washington's Headquarters, is shown clearly in this drawing by E. A. Abbey, published in Harper's Weekly *in June 1873. Courtesy of the Historical Society of Newburgh Bay and the Highlands*

Hugh Walsh, Esq., was born in Ireland in 1745 and lived there uintil 1764. In 1776 he was a resident of New York City, engaged in supplying the Continental Army. After the Revolutionary War he settled in Newburgh, residing on Broadway between Liberty and Grand streets. He died in 1817. Courtesy of the Historical Society of Newburgh Bay and the Highlands

A gravestone at the New Windsor Cantonment, slightly to the south of Newburgh, marks an important Revolutionary War site that was not a battlefield. It was the final campground of the Continental Army in 1782-1783. Photograph by Robert Paul Molay

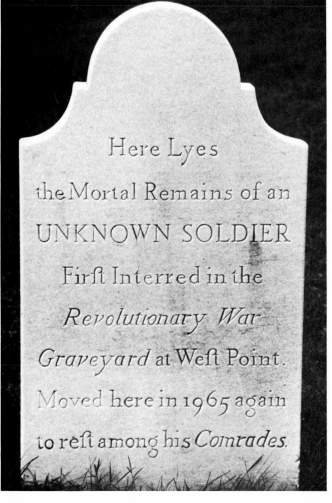

Here Lyes
the Mortal Remains of an
UNKNOWN SOLDIER
First Interred in the
*Revolutionary War
Graveyard* at West Point.
Moved here in 1965 again
to rest among his *Comrades.*

Archaeological work in progress on September 6, 1934, shows the painstaking efforts that were devoted to ruins of original huts occupied by Gen. George Washington's army during the winter of 1782-1783 at the New Windsor Cantonment. Courtesy of the Historical Society of Newburgh Bay and the Highlands

To help visitors visualize the life lived by seven thousand American troops at the New Windsor Cantonment, their final encampment in 1782-1783, the site is staffed today by interpretive assistants in authentic period costumes who perform military drill and demonstrate many other aspects of camp life in the eighteenth century. Photograph by Robert Paul Molay

A group of unidentified participants gathered at the New Windsor Cantonment historic site, probably in the 1930s. Visible are some of the rugged construction details of the so-called Publick Building. Courtesy of the Historical Society of Newburgh Bay and the Highlands

The "first annual pilgrimage" of the Jerusalem Temple Lodge No. 721 F&AM, Cornwall was photographed July 12, 1935, at Temple Hill, site of the 1782-1783 final encampment of the Continental Army in New Windsor, just south of Newburgh. Courtesy of the Historical Society of Newburgh Bay and the Highlands

The Isaac Belknap homestead in Little Britain (New Windsor) is now within the confines of Stewart Airport. It was built about 1770 by Jonathan Belknap, and was eventually purchased by Robert Morrison in 1872. Courtesy of the Historical Society of Newburgh Bay and the Highlands

The John Ellison House in New Windsor was built in 1754, even though this postcard claims it was erected in 1734. The house was important in Revolutionary War history as the headquarters for Gen. Henry Knox on four separate occasions in 1779, 1780, 1781, and 1782. The builder was the legendary Orange County stonemason, William Bull. Courtesy of Key Bank

Headquarters, near Newburg, N.Y. Erected 1734.

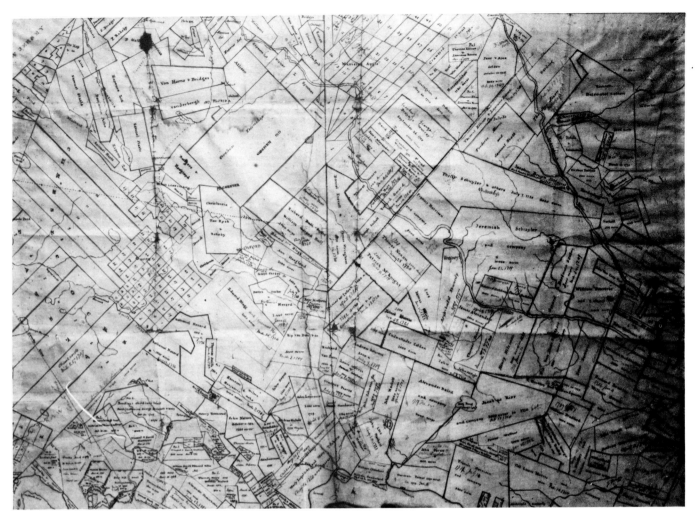

This rare early map of Orange County, New York, shows the principal holdings dating to the early eighteenth century. Courtesy of the Historical Society of Newburgh Bay and the Highlands

The Verplanck House at Plum Point, over-looking the Hudson River at New Windsor, was built by Philip Alexander Verplanck, a descendant of the Gulian VerPlanck who was a founder of the Society of the Cincinnati in 1783. Philip Alexander VerPlanck patterned his mansion after the Greek Temple of Poseidon at Attica, on the promontory of Sunium, the most southerly tip of the Greek mainland overlooking the Aegean Sea. Built in 1838, the mansion was demolished in 1955. Photograph by Walter A. Tuttle, courtesy of the Historical Society of Newburgh Bay and the Highlands

33

The Verplanck mansion as painted by noted local artist John Wilkie Beal, completed on February 27, 1953. Beal, a retired executive of Central Hudson Gas & Electric Corp., has been a painter, cartoonist, writer, and poet for over fifty years. Photograph by Robert Paul Molay

Newburgh Academy was erected in 1796, and was later known as Newburgh Free Academy through its final year of 1886. The name survives today in the public high school that serves the Enlarged Newburgh School District, on Fullerton Avenue. Courtesy of the Historical Society of Newburgh Bay and the Highlands

Famous engraving by the English artist W. G. Wall, from a drawing he made in Newburgh in the 1820s. On the right is Montgomery Street, at the intersection of South Street. The first house on the right, known as the Reeve House, is still standing. It was built between 1800 and 1806 by Selah Reeve, a manufacturer of earthenware. According to one local tradition, the Marquis de Lafayette danced in the Reeve House when he returned to Newburgh for a visit after the successful outcome of the American Revolution. Courtesy of the Historical Society of Newburgh Bay and the Highlands

The residence of J. Walker Fowler at the northeast corner of Liberty and Campbell streets was erected in 1820 as a parsonage for the Rev. James Scringeour, pastor of the First Associate Reformed Church, at the corner of Grand and First streets. Courtesy of the Historical Society of Newburgh Bay and the Highlands

The residence of David Crawford, built in 1830, is one of the most elegant edifices on Newburgh's Montgomery Street—where a unified and careful historical restoration effort has succeeded in recapturing the opulent flavor of life that prevailed in this river city in the nineteenth century. On October 3, 1953, Crawford House was scheduled to be sold at public auction, almost certainly dooming it to demolition or conversion to an apartment house. With only five days left to take decisive action, the Historical Society of Newburgh Bay and the Highlands purchased Crawford House on September 28, 1953. Some early contributors to the purchase fund were the Ossoli Club, the Trustees of Washington's Headquarters, and the Daughters of the American Revolution, Quassaick Chapter. Photograph by Robert Paul Molay

Treasures of Crawford House, preserving for future generations the flavor of nineteenth-century life along the Hudson River, include a candle mold, a spinning wheel and a jointed doll with delicate painted features. Photographs by Robert Paul Molay, courtesy of the Historical Society of Newburgh Bay and the Highlands

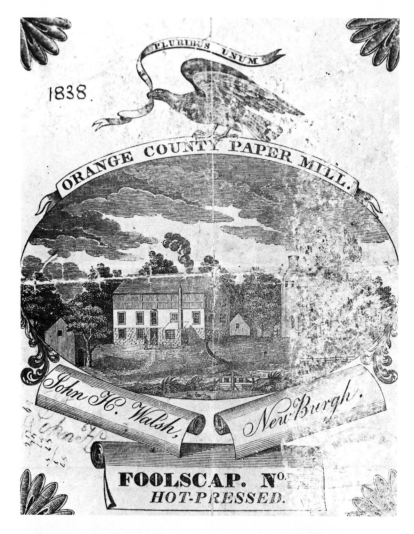

This advertisement for the Orange County Paper Mill of Newburgh has been dated 1838. Courtesy of the Historical Society of Newburgh Bay and the Highlands

Lieutenant General Scott, apparently a Newburgh personality, was portrayed in this rather severe pose by Elias Dexter, 582 Broadway. Courtesy of the Historical Society of Newburgh Bay and the Highlands

Col. Henry Robinson, for whom Newburgh's Robinson Avenue is named, promised his wife a palace. Instead, he spent a fortune building this pyramid-like tomb for himself in the city's Old Towne Burying Ground. He was interred there in 1853. When Mrs. Robinson died, the colonel's promise was fulfilled as she was allowed to be buried in the "palatial" tomb. Photograph by Robert Paul Molay

Quassaick Bank was the customer for a printing job done by the Newburgh Telegraph, as indicated by this receipt for $38.00 dated September 25, 1854. The cut at upper left corner shows Washington's Headquarters and the entrance to the Highlands of the Hudson. Courtesy of the Historical Society of Newburgh Bay and the Highlands

Another receipt, stuck to the Quassaick Bank slip with a blob of sealing wax, shows a view of the Highland Paper Mills. Courtesy of the Historical Society of Newburgh Bay and the Highlands

James A. Townsend was best known as the owner of the Highland Paper Mill, located at the point where the Moodna Creek meets the Hudson River. He came to Newburgh in 1856 at the age of twenty-six and soon became a business associate of Homer Ramsdell. By 1880 he was sole proprietor of a wholesale grocery business at 10 Water Street. Photograph from Portrait and Biographical Record of Orange County, New York

Winter at the shipyard on the Hudson River, below Newburgh, is captured in an old engraving by W. Wellstood, made "expressly for the Ladies Repository." Courtesy of the Historical Society of Newburgh Bay and the Highlands

The photographs of these Civil War soldiers have been preserved but their identities are unknown. Courtesy of the Historical Society of Newburgh Bay and the Highlands

Major H. S. Murray of the 124th New York Regiment, the renowned "Orange Blossoms" of Orange County, was photographed by M. J. Powers at the Whitehurst Gallery, Washington, D.C. Courtesy of the Historical Society of Newburgh Bay and the Highlands

The sadness and human waste of civil war is summed up in a few eloquent words penciled on the reverse side of this faded photograph: "Lieutenant J. Nelson Decker, 'Harris Light Cavalry' fell 17th April 1862 while gallantly leading a gallant charge at Falmouth, Virginia. Buried 19th in Falmouth churchyard. May 3rd he was brought to Newburgh by Sergeant Major Charles S. Joslyn and on the 6th was buried in Newburgh Cemetery. . ." Courtesy of the Historical Society of Newburgh Bay and the Highlands

Another volunteer in the "Orange Blossoms," whose name has been lost, was photographed nearer to home by Pope Brothers of Washington Hall, Newburgh. Courtesy of the Historical Society of Newburgh Bay and the Highlands

A pair of Union soldiers from Newburgh, dressed in mufti, are identified only as Millet and McCarthy. They were in Sutler's 139th New York State Regiment, and photographed by D. C. Maxwell of Lynchburg, Virginia. Courtesy of the Historical Society of Newburgh Bay and the Highlands

Lt. C. B. Caldwell of Newburgh was in the 98th Regiment, New York Volunteers, when he was photographed by Hall & Judkins, near the headquarters of the 24th Army Corps. Courtesy of the Historical Society of Newburgh Bay and the Highlands

The fanciful pastime of posing in tableaux vivants was popular in Newburgh around the time of the Civil War. This group of the Nine Muses is dated April 4 and 5, 1866, People's Hall. The muses are (from left) Miss Welling, Kate Johnston, Gertrude Hardy, Myra Wiltsie, Maggie Masters, Mary Bigler, Nettie S— (illegible), Josie Dusenberry, and Celie G. Howell. Courtesy of the Historical Society of Newburgh Bay and the Highlands

Celia J. Howell played the part of Faith in this tableau from April 5, 1866. Courtesy of the Historical Society of Newburgh Bay and the Highlands

Miss Gertrude Heardy posed as "Temperance" on April 5, 1866. Courtesy of the Historical Society of Newburgh Bay and the Highlands

"*Esther discloses Haman's treachery and pleads for her people.*" *This* tableau vivant, *probably also from April 1866, required the services of Miss Dusenberry, Emma Bigler, Mrs. S. Wiltsie, Miss S—(illegible), Charles Seaman, Isaac C. Chapman, A. T. Wiltsie, and S. Fred Wiltsie. Courtesy of the Historical Society of Newburgh Bay and the Highlands*

Though her name has faded from the back of this photograph and can no longer be deciphered, she is frozen forever in the attitude of Queen Esther, also photographed in April 1866 at the People's Hall. Courtesy of the Historical Society of Newburgh Bay and the Highlands

The Newburgh Tableaux Vivants Association embraced a broad selection of subject matter. Here they have shifted gears from the Old Testament to "The Wooing of Minnetonka." Courtesy of the Historical Society of Newburgh Bay and the Highlands

In this tableau vivant Minnehaha is portrayed by Miss Allie M. Pennoyer, Hiawatha by Charles Lawson, and the second male character by Isaac C. Chapman. Courtesy of the Historical Society of Newburgh Bay and the Highlands

William Roe built the original Roe homestead on Grand Street in Newburgh. Courtesy of the Historical Society of Newburgh Bay and the Highlands

John W. Little, standing, and William J. Roe II in an old miniature photograph. The Roes were early residents of Newburgh's Grand Street. Courtesy of the Historical Society of Newburgh Bay and the Highlands

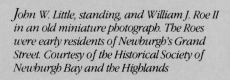

William J. Roe II, photographed again in his later years, was the grandson of the fore-bidding-looking gentleman with the walking stick. Courtesy of the Historical Society of Newburgh Bay and the Highlands

William Hazard Roe, known affectionately as "Uncle Hazzie," lived to the age of 101. Courtesy of the Historical Society of Newburgh Bay and the Highlands

R. V. K. Montfort, M.D., *was one of Newburgh's outstanding teachers and educators in the nineteenth century. While teaching high school in Newburgh he earned his medical degree in 1856. He was elected clerk and superintendent of schools in 1859, a position he held at various times over a period of about forty years. He joined the "Orange Blossoms," the 124th New York Infantry, during the Civil War. Returning to Newburgh in 1865, he became the city's health officer. Dr. Montfort was a staff physician at St. Luke's Hospital until 1892. He was also active in the Ellis Post, Grand Army of the Republic. Photograph from* Portrait and Biographical Record of Orange County, New York

George Clark was Newburgh's first mayor, serving from March 1866 to March 1870. He was born in Newburgh August 7, 1817, to Irish parents. He had developed a friendship with Ulysses S. Grant, who was elected president during Clark's term as mayor and visited Newburgh on August 7, 1869. Among his other civic and commercial interests, Clark was president of the Newburgh & Midland Railroad at the time of his death in 1871. Courtesy of the Historical Society of Newburgh Bay and the Highlands

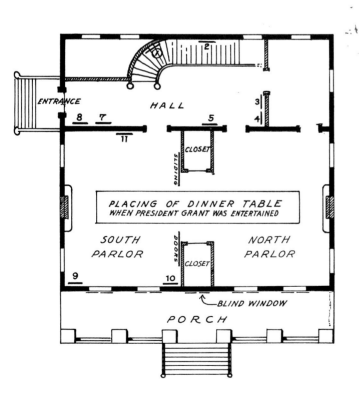

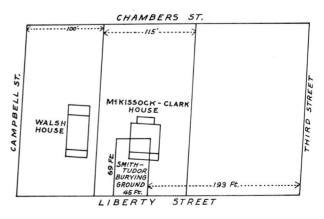

The house on Liberty Street where Mayor Clark lived and entertained President Grant. This photograph is from 1937, before the structure was demolished to make way for the present-day Post Office building. The street map shows the precise location of the McKissock-Clark House, and the floor plan of the house recalls the visit of Ulysses S. Grant. Courtesy of the Historical Society of Newburgh Bay and the Highlands

*Alex Morgan, the first constable of
Newburgh, sat for this faded tintype.
Courtesy of the Historical Society of
Newburgh Bay and the Highlands*

*James Chadwick was president of a
vanished Newburgh landmark, the bleachery
on Lake Street. He was born in England in
1830 and bought the sprawling bleachery site
in 1871. Until his time it had been used as a
flour mill. Water power for the mill was
provided by Muchattoes Lake and the Quassaick Creek, with reserve power available
from Orange Lake. It was a matter of pride
to the bleachery that it used 1,250,000
gallons of pure spring water daily in the
bleaching process. The site was later known
as Tell Industries, punctuated by a tall
smokestack which stood until the beginning
of the current decade. Photograph from*
Portrait and Biographical Record of Orange
County, New York

*William H. Kelly was principal of
Newburgh's Washington Street School from
1861 through 1910. As if forty-nine years on
that assignment were not enough, he went
on to serve for another eleven years, until
1921, as principal of the Broadway School.
Courtesy of the Historical Society of
Newburgh Bay and the Highlands*

David Barclay, a Newburgh landowner in the nineteenth century, was photographed in Madison, Wisconsin. His wife, Christina Eliza (Baird) Barclay, was photographed in middle age by W. W. Whiddit of 108 Water Street, Newburgh, and again in old age by Schaeffer of 275 Main Street, Poughkeepsie. Courtesy of the Historical Society of Newburgh Bay and the Highlands

Col. Wiliam D. Dickey was born in Newburgh January 11, 1845. After service in the Civil War he earned a law degree and threw himself into the affairs of Newburgh with great gusto. He was associated with the trolley company in Newburgh as well as the Newburgh & Orange Lake Electric Street Railway. He and his brother developed the forty acres known as Washington Heights as a residential neighborhood, and chose the lot at the corner of Bay View Terrace and Overlook Place for his own residence. He was the first president of the Newburgh Fire Department and spearheaded the drive beginning in 1892 to construct the elegant Palatine Hotel. Photograph from Portrait and Biographical Record of Orange County, New York

Distinguished scholar E. M. Ruttenber, who wrote definitive histories of Newburgh and Orange County, as portrayed by photographer William Henry Mapes of Newburgh. Courtesy of the Historical Society of Newburgh Bay and the Highlands

This delicate fountain sculpture at 252 Liberty Street was photographed about 1874 in front of a later residence of William D. Dickey, who had then become a judge. Courtesy of the Historical Society of Newburgh Bay and the Highlands

Orange Lake, several miles inland from the Hudson River, was once linked to the city of Newburgh by a trolley line. A postcard shows the former boat house at Orange Lake, with several properly dressed summer canoeists dipping their paddles in the lake. Courtesy of Key Bank

Lt. Charles Hogan was photographed March 24, 1879 by Bogardus Studio of New York City. Courtesy of the Historical Society of Newburgh Bay and the Highlands

The Hon. William Fullerton, whose name is preserved in Fullerton Avenue on Newburgh's West End, lived in Newburgh and practiced law in New York City. He was born in Orange County in 1817. In later life he was one of Chester A. Arthur's intimate friends. He was appointed a justice of the state Supreme Court, to fill a vacancy, in 1867 and later served with distinction on the Court of Appeals. Photograph from Portrait and Biographical Record of Orange County, New York.

The nineteenth-century studio photographers practicing in Newburgh apparently took more pains to preserve their own names than to identify their sitters for posterity. This group of miniatures lacks any surviving information on the subjects. All are 2½ inches by 4 inches, mounted on stiff card stock. The photographers represented in this group are Remillard, 82 Water Street; Lawrence; Le Roy's Gem Gallery, 78 Water Street (Corner of Third); Pope, Washington Hall (duplicates are available if desired); and one establishment outside of Newburgh: Frank Edsall, Goshen, New York. Courtesy of the Historical Society of Newburgh Bay and the Highlands

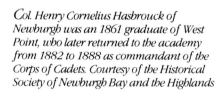

Quassaick National Bank, photographed between 1880 and 1883, was staffed by (from left) Frank Weed, Mr. Camack, Mr. Dickey (barely visible in shadows at center), Mr. Lendeman, and Mr. Mitchell. Courtesy of the Historical Society of Newburgh Bay and the Highlands

Col. Henry Cornelius Hasbrouck of Newburgh was an 1861 graduate of West Point, who later returned to the academy from 1882 to 1888 as commandant of the Corps of Cadets. Courtesy of the Historical Society of Newburgh Bay and the Highlands

CUTTING HER WAY THROUGH THE ICE

COASTING ON 4TH STREET HILL

COMBINING PLEASURE WITH BUSINESS

Frank Leslie's Illustrated Newspaper *of February 28, 1880 showed winter scenes from Newburgh, including the small inset at upper left, captioned: "Ferryboat cutting her way through the ice." Courtesy of the Historical Society of Newburgh Bay and the Highlands*

This miniature photograph by A. Peck of 117 Water Street, Newburgh, bears the penciled notation on its reverse side: Daniel Waring, brother of Alvah Waring. Courtesy of the Historical Society of Newburgh Bay and the Highlands

A view of the Newburgh waterfront in the 1880s shows the side-wheeled steamer John Rome *docked along Water Street. Courtesy of the Historical Society of Newburgh Bay and the Highlands*

Capt. George D. Woolsey was the scion of a distinguished river family originating in Dutchess County. His father, Elijah Woolsey, had been captain of the sloop Intelligence *and the early steamers* Lady Richmond *and* Richard Davis. *The family moved from Poughkeepsie to Newburgh in 1831. Captain Woolsey purchased the sloop* Samsondale *in 1862 and operated it until the end of the nineteenth century. Photograph from* Portrait and Biographical Record of Orange County, New York

Mount Saint Mary's Academy was founded in 1883, under the direction of the Sisters of St. Dominic, and granted a state charter in 1888. Under the leadership of Sister Mary Hildegarde it quickly became one of Newburgh's most prominent educational institutions. The high elevation of the campus along Powell Avenue gives Mount Saint Mary a view of the Hudson River extending for miles. Today Mount Saint Mary is an accredited four-year college for men and women. Photograph from Portrait and Biographical Record of Orange County, New York

Rose Brick Company was established in 1883 on the west bank of the Hudson River, in the town of Newburgh, by Milend C. Rose in partnership with his father, John C. Rose. Their site, chosen for its rich deposits of suitable clay, eventually covered 250 acres and became the largest brickyard on the Hudson. Each of Rose's sixteen machines had a capacity of 24,000 bricks per day, for an average yearly output of 44 million bricks. Rose & Company operated a fleet of seven barges to carry the finished product downriver. Roseton was originally inhabited by many of Rose's four hundred to five hundred workers, and Milend C. Rose was the town's first postmaster. Today Central Hudson Gas and Electric Company operates power plants at Roseton and at the adjacent Danskammer, the Devil's Dance Chamber where Indian rituals were frequently observed by early Dutch visitors. Courtesy of Oliver Shipp

Andrew V. Jova, M.D., was a nephew of John J. Jova, the "brick king" of Roseton, who established a medical practice in Newburgh in 1891. The Jova Brick Works produced millions of bricks bearing the "JJJ" trade-mark from 1885 through 1968. Photograph from Portrait and Biographical Record of Orange County, New York

The riverfront between Broadway and First Street is seen in winter, during the 1880s. Courtesy of the Historical Society of Newburgh Bay and the Highlands

The names of the sitters for this group of tintypes, an obsolete photographic process, have been lost, but the poses and costumes help recapture the flavor of the nineteenth-century life in the Hudson Valley. Courtesy of the Historical Society of Newburgh Bay and the Highlands

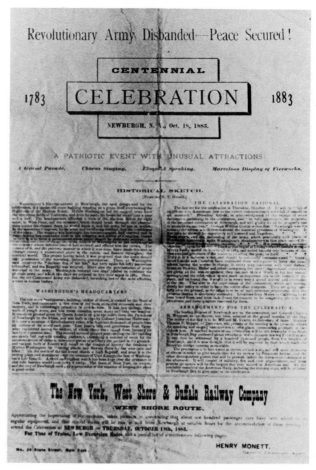

A handbill describes the celebration in Newburgh on October 18, 1883, marking the centennial of the formal cessation of hostilities of the American Revolution. Courtesy of Helen VerNooy Gearn

The October 27, 1883 Harper's Weekly *showed the facade of the 1841 County Court House on Grand Street in patriotic bunting for the centennial celebration in Newburgh marking the official end of the War for Independence. Courtesy of the Historical Society of Newburgh Bay and the Highlands*

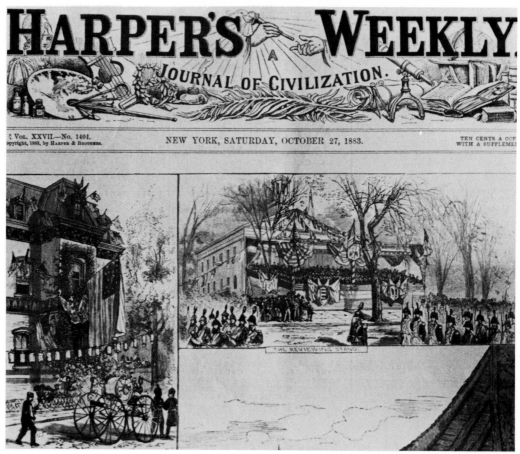

Capt. William Coleman spent his entire life on the Hudson River, piloting sloops, ferries, tugboats, and government boats loaded with dynamite. He was born near Newburgh in 1834. In 1884 he built the tug James J. Logan, *which he operated for many years. He was also one of the original directors of the Columbus Trust Company, now part of Key Bank. Photograph from* Portrait and Biographical Record of Orange County, New York

This fanciful stone stable building, shown in an 1884 photograph, was originally the property of Newburgh's beloved Andrew Jackson Downing, whose views on landscape gardening, country living and public parks dominated the tastes of nineteenth-century Hudson Valley esthetes. The property was later known as the Grace Alger Place and after that was owned by the Hon. William W. Carson. The building was removed in 1927. Courtesy of the Historical Society of Newburgh Bay and the Highlands

A faded photograph from the 1880s bears the title "Coal Dock & The Old Crib." It shows a now-vanished section of the Newburgh riverfront. Courtesy of the Historical Society of Newburgh Bay and the Highlands

The only information that has been preserved about this baseball team of long-ago Newburgh is that the group included the twins, Tom and Bill Martin, one of them a Newburgh policeman. Courtesy of the Historical Society of Newburgh Bay and the Highlands

The first edition of the Newburgh Daily News *made its bow to the world on September 5, 1885, with its publication office at 126 Broadway. Describing itself as "A One-Cent Newspaper—Independent, but not neutral," the* Daily News *was published by William H. Keefe. Courtesy of Robert Mancinelli*

NEWBURGH DAILY NEWS

Vol. 1--No. 1. | PUBLICATION OFFICE | IN BROADWAY | NEWBURGH, N. Y., SATURDAY EVENING, SEPTEMBER 5, 1885. | PRICE, ONE CENT.

"I WILL KILL YOU AND HIM, TOO."

Miss Westcott tells a Coroner's Jury about Dr. Curry's Attempt to Kill Her.

RED BANK, Sept. 4.—The inquest into the cause of the death of Dr. George H. Curry, who shot himself after attempting to kill Miss Susie Westcott, was held this afternoon by Coroner R. T. Smith and a jury. Miss Susie Westcott was the first witness. Her testimony corroborated the story already published, except as to her interview with Dr. Curry after he led her to the dark end of the piazza, Miss Westcott said:

"Dr. Curry pulled me rudely off the porch and said, 'Will you marry me tomorrow?' I said 'No. Then you love someone else,' he said. 'I do,' I replied. Then drawing a revolver, Dr. Curry said: 'I will kill you and him, too.' He fired at me and the ball struck my corset steel and was flatened, doing me no real injury.

Miss Westcott also testified that once when she and Dr. Curry were sitting together down by the river he took a pistol from his pocket and, placing the muzzle against his forehead, said: "Shall I shoot?" Thinking he was only joking she said: "Yes, if you want to." Dr. Curry laughed and put his pistol away.

William H. Steven made a long statement, in which he spoke of Dr. Curry as acting very strangely on the Monday afternoon before the shooting. He told how Dr. Curry had proposed that they should go up to Newman Springs and have a mock duel before Miss Westcott. "We will shoot at each other with blank cartridges," said Curry, "and at a explosion I will put my hand to my forehead and exclaim: 'I am shot,' at the same time making a red mark with a red composition which I shall have in my hand for that purpose. This will frighten Miss Westcott and bring her around."

The jury after a minute's deliberation returned the following verdict.

"Dr. Curry came to his death by a pistol-shot wound inflicted by his own hand."

Misses Susie and Carrie Westcott went to see Mrs. Curry immediately after the inquest. Mrs. Curry said tonight that she has no ill feeling against Miss Westcott.

DESTITUTION IN ELIZABETHPORT.

700 Employees of the Cordage Works Thrown Out of Employment.

Two months ago, the immense cordage works at Elizabethport, N. J., shut down, and the employees, to the number of 700, were informed that work would be resumed on Sept. 1. The reason given for the suspension of manufacture was that a heavy order from the Russian government had been cancelled, and that the stock on hand was entirely too heavy to warrant making up more. A few of the workmen left Elizabethport and sought employment in other places, but most of them waited impatiently for the promised resumption of work on the first of this month. Work has not been resumed, and Superintendent Fulton cannot tell when it will be, consequently the men are in despair and on the verge of destitution. Further credit has been refused to most of them by the grocer and butcher, who aver that to carry them any longer will result in ruin.

The workmen say that owing to the low rate of wages paid when the works were running, most of them were unable to save any money, and now they see nothing ahead but starvation or an appeal to public charity. The cordage works are among the largest in the country and have been running without interruption for years.

DEATH OF THE FAT WOMAN.

Said to Be the Largest of Her Sex—The Mammoth Coffin.

PHILADELPHIA, Sept. 4.—Mrs. Emma M. Markley, who is credited with being the heaviest woman in the country, was buried from her home, 526 Lombard street, to-day. She was known to the amusement public as Mme. Victoria. Her advertised weight was over 600 pounds and her actual weight about 550 pounds. She was born in Reading, Pa., about thirty-three years ago, and was slim and delicate throughout her girlhood. At 19 she weighed ninety pounds only, but from this age began to gradually gain flesh. Between three and five years ago when she made an application for an insurance policy, she weighed 289 pounds. Afterward her weight increased rapidly, until she gained the distinction of being the fattest woman in the country, if not in the world.

Runaway of a Hook and Ladder.

CORONA, N. Y., Sept. 4.—For the first time in his life P. J. Dwyer jumped on a hook and ladder truck this afternoon when an alarm of fire sounded and took his place at the wheel. As they were nearing a turn Driver George Wisely gave instructions to Dwyer how to manage the wheel, but he was inexperienced and the hind wheel of the truck swung to the sidewalk, smashed a carriage, and the ladders tore off a window sash and blinds of the Rakin block. The horse started on a run and the tillerman lost control, and the truck swung to the opposite side of the street and tore off several stoops. Then the fences suffered and Dwyer was thrown to the ground and severely injured. The driver was thrown from his seat twice, but clung to the lines till the truck upset. He was dragged some distance by the horses. The horses were finally captured, but while being taken to the stable they ran away again. The damage will reach several hundred dollars. The fire board are investigating, and discharges are probable.

A Philadelphia Druggist's Mistake.

PHILADELPHIA, Sept. 4.—Milton Ogden of West Philadelphia, who was suffering from catarrh went to S. E. Betts's drug store, at Thirty-sixth and Wallace streets, one Saturday night, and asked for vita suppositories. On opening the box it was found to contain six small bottles filled with white powder. He smelled some of it in one of his nostrils and immediately gave vent to piercing shrieks. The druggist was sent for and discovered that the drug was verbane, a deadly poison. A policeman carried the boy upstairs and says he was the hardest person to manage he ever had hold of, although he is not larger than an ordinary twelve-year-old boy. It required three men to hold him on the bed. To-day he was insane but quieted down somewhat at night. The druggist blames the mistake on the manufacturer in New York.

Ruined by Policy and Lottery Playing.

LOUISVILLE, Sept. 4.—Joseph Heim, shoe manufacturer and merchant, is missing. Suits were filed against him to-day charging that he has left the State to defraud his creditors. He is the treasurer of both the St. Charles Benevolent Society and St. Martin's Brotherhood and was a leading member of several other German societies. It is charged that he has taken several thousand dollars belonging to these organizations with him. He leaves also a number of creditors. He left home on Tuesday by way of the back door, and has not been seen by his family since. Policy and lottery playing are said to have been the cause of Heim's downfall.

A Man of Forty Marries a Girl of Ten.

ATLANTA, Sept. 4.—To-day a most extraordinary wedding occurred in Pierce county, Georgia. Wilfiel Harrel, aged 40, a resident of that county, espoused Sallie Wilson, aged only ten and a half years. The girl's father is ferryman for Major Spence, and gave consent to the wedding. The couple went to Macon on their wedding tour, and return home to begin housekeeping to-morrow. All the parties are white and are well connected.

Second Attempt Successful.

NEWARK, Sept. 4.—Stephen Belknap, the Newark stenographer, who recently took ten dover powders and recovered in a hospital, was found drowned in the Passaic River at Belleville to-night. He rode out to Belleville this afternoon on a horse car, and got off at the bridge, where he was last seen crossing the river.

Albany Republicans for Dr. Swinburne.

ALBANY, Sept. 4.—The Republican General Committee to-night called Assembly conventions and primaries. A resolution was adopted urging upon the Republicans of the State the nomination of Dr. John Swinburne for Governor, believing that such selection will be a sure harbinger of victory in November.

A Hard-Hearted Rink Manager.

Harry Tufts, the bicycle rider, who married Miss Pauline Clark, daughter of Erie Engineer James Clark, of Port Jervis, lost his three-months-old child last week. Mr. Tuft and wife were stopping at Coney Island, and he had an engagement at a rink at Bayshore, L. I., for Wednesday night. When the child died he telegraphed the manager asking to be released, saying he would give a free exhibition at a later date. The manager, who could not distinguish between warm charity and cold business, refused to release him from his engagement, and he went to Bayshore and gave the exhibition, leaving his wife to watch alone over the dead form of their child. The hard-hearted manager's course has called for considerable criticism. The story is told at length in the Rink and Roller, a journal devoted to rink entertainments, and is being copied throughout the country. Mr. and Mrs. Tufts are well known here, he having given several exhibitions in this city.

Will Not Flourish Like the Bay Tree.

It is reported that a number of blooming maidens of Port Jervis, ranging all the way from sixteen to twenty-five years, have formed a society and that they propose to give a series of dances during the Winter among themselves. It is also said the first dance occurred Tuesday evening at the residence of one of the lady members and that in accordance with the rules of the society no gentlemen were present. It won't last. Young ladies long for the presence of their gentlemen friends on such occasions, just as much as the latter are pleased when in ladies' society. 'Tis human nature.

Benjamin B. Odell, Jr., born in Newburgh in 1854, was the son of the steamship entrepreneur and industrialist who had interests throughout the Mid-Hudson Valley. After college, he joined his father in the ice business and became secretary and treasurer of the Muchattoes Lake Ice Company in 1886. Two years later he became president of the Newburgh Electric Light and Power Company. Photograph from Portrait and Biographical Record of Orange County, New York

Another son of Benjamin B. Odell was Hiram Odell, born August 21, 1856, in Newburgh. Like his brother, he was associated with Muchattoes Lake Ice Company and the Newburgh Electric Light and Power Company. Photograph from Portrait and Biographical Record of Orange County, New York

This grocery store at the corner of Washington and William streets in Newburgh was constructed by George W. Fuller, a native of the city, in 1888. Fuller had worked in the coal trade along the Hudson River and had also been employed as collector on the Newburgh & Fishkill ferry before starting at the bottom of the grocery business. His building at 192 Washington Street was known as The Business Block. Engraving from Portrait and Biographical Record of Orange County, New York

A school class group from Newburgh was taken in June 1888 or 1889 by photographer J. C. Le Roy. The price to these seventh graders was fifty cents per print. Courtesy of the Historical Society of Newburgh Bay and the Highlands

This view shows Homer Ramsdell & Co. docks at Newburgh in the 1880s. The boats in the foreground are identified as belonging to a Jimmy Hopper. Courtesy of the Historical Society of Newburgh Bay and the Highlands

The Old Dell House, formerly the Riverside Hotel, once stood at the northeast corner of Front and Second streets in Newburgh. It was razed in the late 1890s, to create an open plaza around the new ferry terminal constructed in 1899. Standing in the doorway of the Dell House is "Cokey" Harris, who drove a baggage express wagon. Seated in the horse-drawn rig at right are Fred Baker, agent for Swift & Co. meat packers, and Alex Jeffreys, a horseshoer and blacksmith who carried the unofficial title of Mayor of Front Street. Trolley tracks are visible in the right foreground. Courtesy of the Historical Society of Newburgh Bay and the Highlands

The Class of June 1888 at Newburgh's South Street School, with schoolmaster Elisha Yale Clark at rear, center. Top row, from left: Hudson B. Moore, Nora Seymour, Ada Givens, Mabel Everett, Minnie Hawes, Alice T. Brown, William Hammersly, Alex Davis. Third row, from left: Archie McMillan, Joseph Harrison, Ida Stern, Louis Brown, William Mosher, May Burnett, Anna Purdy, Fred Wooster, William Galloway. Second row, *from left: Charles Mosher, (illegible) Mapes, James Wilkinson, James Voorhees, Raymond Jerome Magee, Bessie Parks, Alida Pickens, Fred Theall. Front row, from left: Alilda Carpenter, Ada Legg, Mabel Latta, Carrie Walsh, N. Deyo Belknap, George Powles, Isaac Goodman, and Raymond Miller. Courtesy of the Historical Society of Newburgh Bay and the Highlands*

William D. Traphagen was descended from the old Dutch stock of Ulster County. He was born in New Hurley, near Kingston, October 21, 1852. For two years, until he was fifteen, Traphagen worked at a dull job as a dry-goods clerk in Newburgh. In 1869 he felt the urge to sign on a whaling vessel out of New Bedford, Massachusetts. During the three-year voyage he was promoted to harpooner. After another long whaling voyage he finally settled down to the shoe business in New-burgh in 1876. By 1891 he was sole proprie-tor of a handsome bootery at 2 Colden Street. Photograph from Portrait and Biographical Record of Orange County, New York

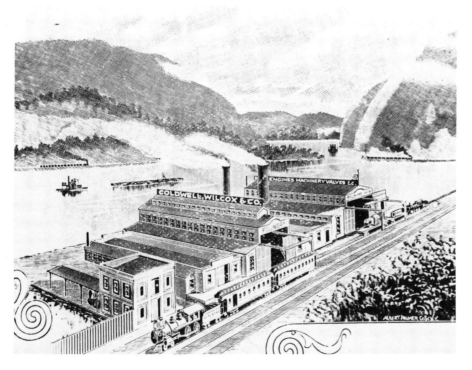

Coldwell, Wilcox & Co. was one of Newburgh's most important industries. Organized in 1884 by Thomas Coldwell, G. R. M. Wilcox, and William H. Coldwell, their original product line was general machinery, fancy ironwork, and steam heat-ing installations for buildings. After five years in operation and several moves to larger quarters, they built a plant along the West Shore Railroad on the New Windsor riverfront. After 1889 their specialty became heavy machinery such as gate valves and sluice gates for dams. Engraving from Portrait and Biographical Record of Orange County, New York

75

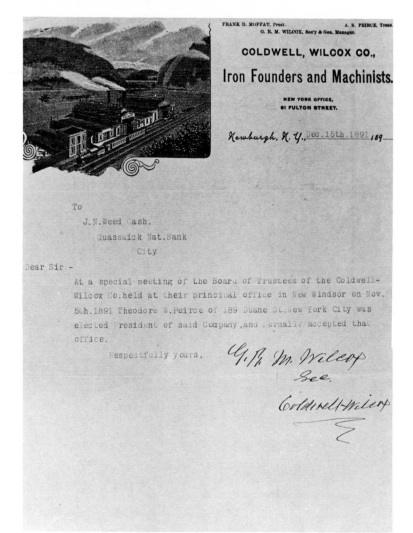

Coldwell, Wilcox & Co. became financially embarrassed in 1890, necessitating a reorganization of the corporation. In its new incarnation it became Coldwell-Wilcox Company, without the "&." This original stock certificate issued to Mrs. Mary E. Pierce on August 6, 1890, is from the era of reorganization and reflects the new corporate name. Courtesy of the Historical Society of Newburgh Bay and the Highlands

The Coldwell-Wilcox plant was destroyed by fire on May 7, 1891, but was soon rebuilt on an even larger scale. A letter in the collection of the Historical Society of Newburgh Bay and the Highlands indicates that Theodore W. Peirce was elected president of the company on November 5, 1891. Among other products made in the new Windsor plant was sugar machinery which was exported to Cuba. Courtesy of the Historical Society of Newburgh Bay and the Highlands

THE WINNING YACHT "SCUD."

THE PRIZE "CUP."

THE "LADY OF THE LAKE" ROUNDING STAKE.

Frank Leslie's Illustrated Newspaper *for February 21, 1891, devoted extensive space to depictions of winter sports on the Hudson River at Newburgh. Courtesy of the Historical Society of Newburgh Bay and the Highlands*

Capt. J. Alfred Walker, born in 1847, was in command of the tugboat R. G. Davis *after 1891. Powered by steam, the tug had a cylinder of fourteen square inches and a keel of fifty-five feet. The* R. G. Davis *was a familiar sight on the stretch of the Hudson River between Newburgh and Kingston. Photograph from* Portrait and Biographical Record of Orange County, New York

Robert Brown's greenhouses were the largest in Newburgh at the end of the nineteenth century, with twenty thousand square feet of glass. The retail business and showroom was located at 49 Second Street. A native of Scotland, Brown is credited with introducing the Chelsea Gem geranium to the United States. Engraving from Portrait and Biographical Record of Orange County, New York

ROBERT BROWN FLORIST.

The front page from the Newburgh Daily Journal *for May 6, 1893, features an advertisement in the righthand column for "Daniel Irwin, Ship Chandler and Sail Maker, 62 South Water Street." Close interrelation between river cities in the Mid-Hudson Valley is shown by the ad at center for "Po'Keepsie Cream" crackers, "The Most Popular Cracker Made in the Country." The* Journal *was produced at 44-46 Second Street. Courtesy Robert Paul Molay*

An elaborate lodge stood at the entrance to the residence of Homer Ramsdell in Newburgh. The overall view was taken in 1893 by "B. M. A.," and the detail of the vaulted arch is from 1894. Courtesy of the Historical Society of Newburgh Bay and the Highlands

The Van Cleft Building on lower Broadway in Newburgh, as it appeared the year it was opened in 1893. The photograph, from the collection of Dr. Robert G. Bull, Marlboro, New York, was donated to the Historical Society of Newburgh Bay and the Highlands in 1979. Courtesy of the Historical Society of Newburgh Bay and the Highlands

A late nineteenth-century view of Newburgh's Front Street is seen on this billhead of the Washington Baking Powder Company dated March 30, 1894. Newburgh had its Washington Street, Washington Terrace, Hotel Washington, Washington Heights—so it is not surprising that a baking powder manufacturer in Newburgh should also choose George Washington as its trademark. Courtesy of Sal Brancato's Village Pizza

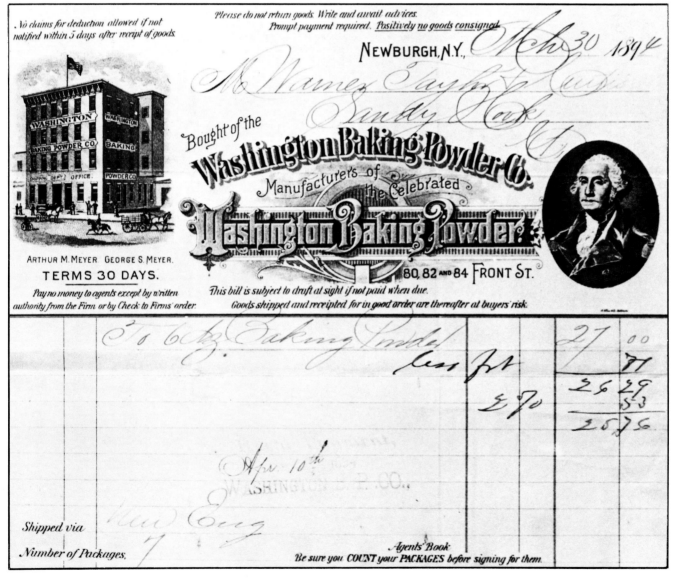

The residence and dairy farm of Wilbur F. Weyant was in New Windsor, four miles south of Newburgh. Engraving from Portrait and Biographical Record of Orange County, New York

The Townsend Dress, a wedding gown worn by Lena Hinchman of Middletown on October 18, 1894, is trimmed with hundreds of seed pearls. Like many of the antique gowns in the collection of the Historical Society of Newburgh Bay and the Highlands, the Townsend Dress is a size 3—far too small to be worn by any uncorseted model of today. Photograph by Robert Paul Molay, courtesy of the Historical Society of Newburgh Bay and the Highlands

Eleanor J. Mackie, a distinguished educator, conducted her school for girls, otherwise known as Quassaick Hall, from 1865 to 1906. She was helped by her five sisters, giving rise to the quaint title of The Misses Mackie School. Eleanor Mackie died on May 14, 1909. Courtesy of the Historical Society of Newburgh Bay and the Highlands

The Misses Mackie's School offered a seven-year classical course, preparing the daughters of prominent Newburgh-area families for admission to the best eastern colleges. The school opened at a location on Chambers Street in 1866, with thirty pupils, then moved in 1867 to a site known as the Leslie House. In 1884 the Mackie sisters moved again to 160 Grand Street, the build-ing in the background of the 1894 class picture by William Henry Mapes, Artist & Photographer of 64 Water Street. Back row (from far left): Hannah Travers, Frances Travers, Mildred Deyo, Pauline Ramsdell Odell, Frances Allen, Edith Deyo, Helen Kerr Collingwood. Middle row (from left): Muriel Youmans (in white), Cornelia Whitehill, Miss Badeau (the teacher), Elsie Chapman, Mabel Dotzert, Camilla Treadwell (of Albany), Gertrude Newlin (of Beacon), Margaret Haight (of Beacon), Bessie Whitehill (with bangs, in white dress), Lulu Cameron, Jessie VanDuzer (of Vails Gate), Theodora Coldwell (in white lace bertha), Louise Cleveland, Rita Chadwick and Olive Wilson (in white). Courtesy of the Historical Society of Newburgh Bay and the Highlands

Newburgh Free Academy, still the proud name of the Newburgh School District's public high school, was located at 123 Chamber Street when this group photograph of the NFA faculty was taken on May 15, 1899. From left to right, foreground, the teachers are Elizabeth Stocker (dark dress), Elizabeth Connelly, J. N. Crane, principal; Anna Fielding, Elsie B. Scott. Sitting in the back were Henry Chandler, Mary Kellogg, an unknown lady, toward the middle, Agnes McFadden, George C. Smith, Ida C. LeRoy, Anna Decker (toward the middle), William J. Woods, and Jennie Carmichael. Courtesy of the Historical Society of Newburgh Bay and the Highlands

This postcard shows the view from Newburgh's Downing Park, looking southward down the Hudson River toward the entrance to Newburgh Bay. Courtesy of Key Bank

Newburgh's Water Street, with an unusually full complement of sidewalk superintendents, is shown in this view taken around 1900 and donated to the historical society by Walter Eggleston in 1957. Courtesy of the Historical Society of Newburgh Bay and the Highlands

This photograph of a trolley on Water Street, taken about 1900, was donated to the historical society by Walter Eggleston in 1957. Courtesy of the Historical Society of Newburgh Bay and the Highlands

Chapman's Bakery was at the intersection of Water and Second streets, in this view from around the turn of the century. Courtesy of the Historical Society of Newburgh Bay and the Highlands

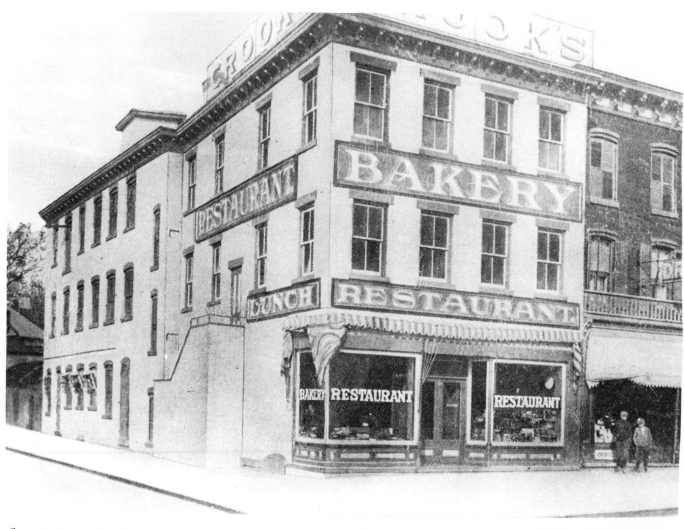

Crook's Bakery and lunchroom, date
unknown, is the subject of this postcard.
Courtesy of Key Bank

This dapper group of musicians was known
as the Mozart String Quartette of Newburgh,
with A. E. Wegle, director. Photo by Peck's
Studio, courtesy of the Historical Society of
Newburgh Bay and the Highlands

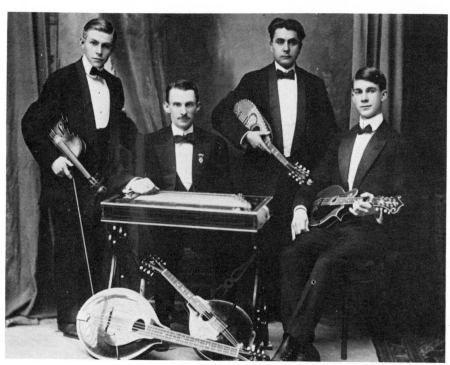

A familiar sight to generations of Mid-Hudson Valley residents was the slips of the Newburgh-Beacon ferry service, at the foot of Second Street in Newburgh. This postcard shows the Newburgh riverfront as seen when approaching from the Beacon side of the river. The ferry was doomed by the opening of the Newburgh-Beacon Bridge in 1963. Courtesy of Key Bank

Ferry service between Newburgh and the east shore of the Hudson River was initiated by Alexander Colden, who obtained the necessary permission from George Clark, lieutenant governor of the colony, on May 24, 1743. Originally landing at Fishkill, the fare was 2 shillings 6 pence for a man and a horse; for a horse or other single animal, 1 shilling 6 pence; for a calf or hog, 6 pence; 6 pence for a firkin (tub) of butter; 6 pence per hundredweight of iron; and 6 shillings for a cart or wagon.

The rates were raised in 1782 when the new Continental public ferry was built. The photograph here shows the twentieth-century version of the ferry, crossing from Beacon to Newburgh. Courtesy of the Historical Society of Newburgh Bay and the Highlands

The Newburgh-Beacon ferry terminal was constructed in 1899, the year of this photograph by A. Templeton, looking north along Front Street. Courtesy of the Historical Society of Newburgh Bay and the Highlands

Another view of the Newburgh-Beacon ferry terminal building, taken by A. E. Templeton on April 8, 1899, looks eastward down Second Street toward the Hudson River. Noteworthy details are the electric-arc street lamp suspended over the intersection and the shod foot at far left, evidently waiting for a shoe shine. Courtesy of the Historical Society of Newburgh Bay and the Highlands

A front view of the Newburgh-Beacon Ferry terminal building was taken by an unidentified photographer, also apparently in 1899. The signs indicate that the traveler could find a variety of services here, including telegraph office, messengers, railroad tickets, cabs, livery stable, and even piano moving. Courtesy of the Historical Society of Newburgh Bay and the Highlands

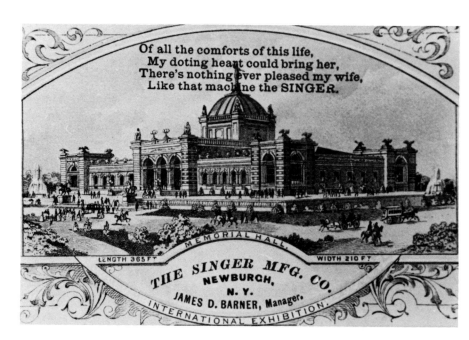

Singer sewing machines, known all over the world, were manufactured in Newburgh beginning around 1900, in a plant at 120 Water Street. These advertising cards carried the fame of Newburgh to an international exhibition in which the Singer Manufacturing Company participated. Courtesy of the Historical Society of Newburgh Bay and the Highlands

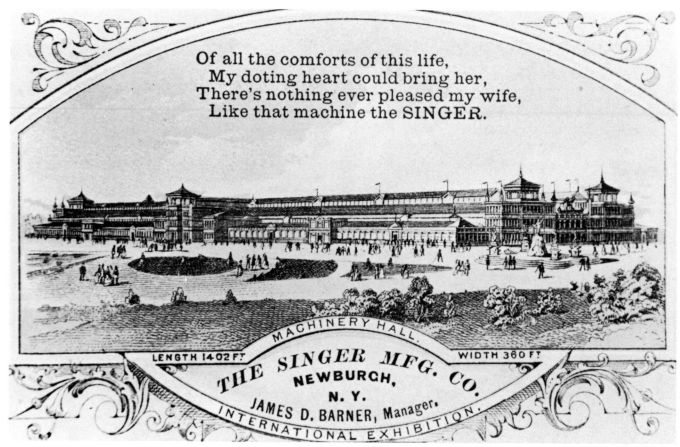

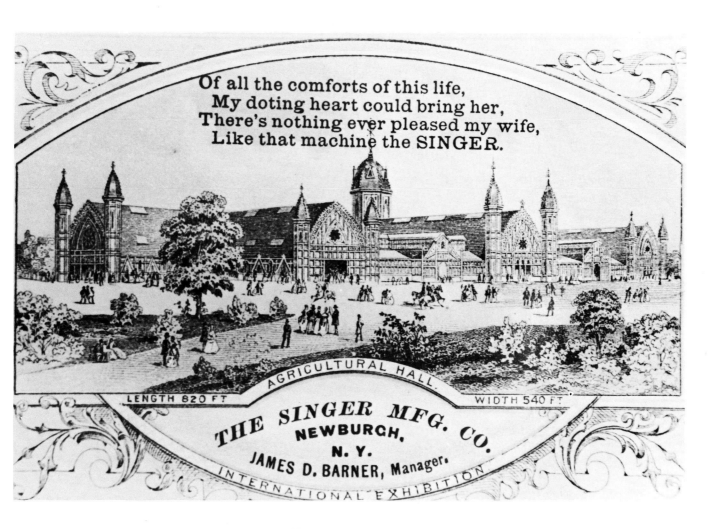

Of all the comforts of this life,
My doting heart could bring her,
There's nothing ever pleased my wife,
Like that machine the SINGER.

AGRICULTURAL HALL.
LENGTH 820 FT
WIDTH 540 FT
THE SINGER MFG. CO.
NEWBURGH,
N.Y.
JAMES D. BARNER, Manager.
INTERNATIONAL EXHIBITION

The Powelton Hotel, located near the present site of the Powelton Club in the north end of Newburgh, was at a later time used as a girls' school. Courtesy of the Historical Society of Newburgh Bay and the Highlands

*A view of Newburgh's First Street, taken in
the horse-and-buggy era, looks east from
Smith Street. Courtesy of the Historical
Society of Newburgh Bay and the Highlands*

Under the leadership of Joseph Van Cleft, the Columbus Trust Company originally opened for business on March 1, 1893, in the Academy of Music building at 82 Broadway. Benjamin B. Odell, Sr., was the bank's first president. The company had outgrown its original quarters by 1901 and purchased an existing building across the street at 78 Broadway. In 1900, the date of this photograph, the building had stores on the street level and apartments upstairs. Courtesy of Key Bank

The lobby of The Columbus Trust Company was a showplace of period elegance when it opened its doors at 78 Broadway in Newburgh on April 29, 1902. Constructed by Joseph M. and William D. Dickey, 78 Broadway once housed Robert Whitehill's Newburgh Steam Engine Works. Columbus Trust Company is now a part of Key Bank, but the building at 78 Broadway still maintains its graceful presence, steps away from the new Key Bank corporate headquarters building overlooking the Hudson River. Courtesy of Key Bank

The former Charles Corley Estate was in the vicinity of St. Francis Roman Catholic Church in New Windsor. According to notes by Rosena N. Neely, the house was burned when a painter used a torch unwisely to remove paint from a wooden area near the roof. Courtesy of the Historical Society of Newburgh Bay and the Highlands

The facade of Calvary Presbyterian Church on South Street, Newburgh, appears in this postcard bearing the handwritten date, October 10, 1906. Courtesy of Key Bank

A slightly different point of view shows the Calvary Presbyterian Church looking south from Farrington Street. Photograph by L. L. Le Roy, courtesy of the Historical Society of Newburgh Bay and the Highlands

This postcard published by J. Ruben, 39 Johnston Street, Newburgh, shows the Columbus Trust Company prior to 1907, when it expanded eastward to incorporate the adjoining building at 76 Broadway. Courtesy of Key Bank

The Rev. William K. Hall, D.D., was pastor of the First Presbyterian Church in Newburgh for thirty-four years. He died September 17, 1906. Courtesy of the Historical Society of Newburgh Bay and the Highlands

The Columbus Trust Company in Newburgh is seen as it appeared some time between June 16, 1902—when the illuminated clock was installed over the doorway at 78 Broadway—and 1907, when the bank completed its eastward expansion by merging with the adjoining building at 76 Broadway (here occupied by a piano dealer). Photograph by J. Ruben, courtesy of Key Bank

Looking south on Newburgh's Grand Street, a horse in harness at the extreme left helps establish the approximate period for this postcard. Courtesy of Key Bank

C. A. PALMER,
Landscape and Mechanical
PHOTOGRAPHER.

Views of Residences, Landscapes, Machinery, &c.; also Publisher of Stereoscopic Views of Hudson River Scenery and general Vicinity Views.

ORDERS SOLICITED.

P. O. Box, 281.   Matteawan, N. Y.

A photographer's business card recalls the days of the stereoscope viewer that was once found in every fashionable Victorian parlor, It also recalls the days when Beacon, directly across the Hudson River from Newburgh, was known as Matteawan. Courtesy of the Historical Society of Newburgh Bay and the Highlands

The Coldwell lawn mower, one of Newburgh's best known manufactured products, is shown here in use by James Henry Dubois and his horse, Nelly. Dubois worked for Mr. and Mrs. Jonathan Thomas on their twelve-acre parcel in Balmville. In return for his labors, Dubois received the use of the horse, produce from the farm, and thirty dollars a month. Courtesy of Margery Shipp

Another photograph of James Henry Dubois shows him with the coach horses, Tom and Jerry. In addition to his duties as full-time gardener for the Thomas family, Dubois was also the coachman—in uniform. Courtesy of Margery Shipp

St. John's Church, Newburgh, is pictured in this postcard. Courtesy of Key Bank

East Coldenham Toll Gate guarded the north side of Cochecton Turnpike, the modern New York State Route 17K, near the old Newburgh city line. A chain was stretched across the road to stop wagons from passing through when the gate was closed. This structure was razed around 1900 and the site was later occupied by the Lily of France lingerie factory. A recollection by Harry H. Hurd of Cochecton Turnpike, dated August 29, 1947, identifies the man in the vest at right as Abraham Rose, the gatekeeper, and his bearded companion as Rose's father-in-law, Mr. Miller. Courtesy of the Historical Society of Newburgh Bay and the Highlands

Newburgh and Cochecton Turnpike was a plank road chartered in 1800, on the route of present-day New York State Route 17K. The last tollgate in the Newburgh vicinity, at East Coldenham, was torn down about 1900, leaving hostelries such as George Stott's Cochecton Hotel for the weary traveler. Courtesy of the Historical Society of Newburgh Bay and the Highlands

Alex Goldberg's haberdashery at 85 Water Street was typical of the fine-quality shops that once lined this busy business artery facing Newburgh's Hudson River frontage. As long as there was passenger service on the West Shore rail line, river steamers stopping at Newburgh Landing, and ferry service from Newburgh to Beacon, Water Street was one of the most important shopping meccas in the entire Mid-Hudson region. This photograph was printed by the author from an undated glass plate negative in the collection of the historical society. Courtesy of the Historical Society of Newburgh Bay and the Highlands

Interior view of Alex Goldberg's men's furnishings shop at 83 Water Street was also printed by the author from an antique eight-by-ten-inch glass plate negative in the collection of the historical society. The interior lighting arrangement is a transitional combination of gaslight fixtures and electric illumination. Although the exact date of this photograph is not known, Thomas Alva Edison had chosen Newburgh as the site for his second electric generating plant (after Pearl Street in New York City), and the power station on Montgomery Street went into operation in 1894. Courtesy of the Historical Society of Newburgh Bay and the Highlands

Newburgh Auction Mart, at 71, 73, and 75 Chamber Street (corner of Campbell Street) advertised "Sale Every Tuesday: Horses, Wagons & Harness." This was the family business of Jerry Shapiro, husband of Mayor Joan Shapiro, and the same building from which he still operates Jerry Shapiro's Discount Furniture Barn. Interesting fea-

tures of this photograph are the unpaved streets and the early carbon-arc street lamp suspended overhead at right. The photograph was printed by the author from an antique glass plate negative in the collection of the historical society. Courtesy of the Historical Society of Newburgh Bay and the Highlands

Fullerton Post, Grand Army of the Republic, posed for this group photograph in Newburgh. Although the distinguished veteran at center is wearing a Union Army cap and the other men in the picture are sporting a variety of interesting headgear, no other information about this photograph has been preserved. Courtesy of the Historical Society of Newburgh Bay and the Highlands

The Frontenac, one of the rarest of early automobiles, was manufactured in Newburgh from 1906 through 1912. The photograph shows the main assembly plant building. Courtesy of Helen VerNooy Gearn

Dr. John T. Howell was born near Middletown, New York, and practiced medicine in Newburgh from 1887 to 1937. His home and office were at 205 Grand Street. This photograph was taken in 1908. His wife, Sarah Townsend Steele, lived from 1864 to 1951. Her family had lived in Cornwall for many generations and owned a cotton mill. Courtesy of the Historical Society of Newburgh Bay and the Highlands

The building at 205 Grand Street, at the corner of Smith Street, where Dr. Howell lived and practiced, was built before 1830 in the early square-brick style. In the 1880s it was Mrs. Bodine's Select Boarding House. Courtesy of the Historical Society of Newburgh Bay and the Highlands

The Newburgh Wheelman's Club, for bicyclists, was organized around 1886. When membership swelled to over three hundred, the club built the rugged stone building on Grand Street that is now owned by St. Patrick's Church. This group photograph was taken January 5, 1911, at the club's annual banquet and was given to the historical society by Walter Eggleston in 1957. Courtesy of the Historical Society of Newburgh Bay and the Highlands

The junction of Grand and Water streets in Newburgh is shown in this postcard view taken in the early days of the automobile age. Courtesy of Key Bank

Daughters of the American Revolution Quassaick Chapter, performed in the play The Home Defenders *on February 10, 1912. The group was photographed in Newburgh by J. Ruben. Courtesy of the Historical Society of Newburgh Bay and the Highlands*

Ringgold Hose Company No. 1, at 63 Colden Street in Newburgh, had joined the horseless-carriage age by the time this photograph was taken. In 1908 the company was still horse-propelled when it entered into a famous race with an automobile. With firefighter Tommy Balfe at the reins, the three-minute race was a tie. Courtesy of Key Bank

Theodore Roosevelt's portrait hangs in the place of honor on the facade of the 1841 Newburgh courthouse, viewed here from Grand Street. Two smaller posters on the central columns depict distinguished statesman Charles Evans Hughes, providing a clue to the approximate date of this photograph. Roosevelt was elected president in 1904, and Hughes was elected governor of the state of New York in 1905. In the 1912 presidential election, Roosevelt lost to Woodrow Wilson; in 1916 it was Hughes who lost to Wilson by the slimmest of margins. The print was made from an original glass plate negative. Courtesy of the Historical Society of Newburgh Bay and the Highlands

Another view of Second Street in Newburgh looks eastward to the Hudson River, with Beacon on the opposite shore. At right is the Newburgh Post Office, surrounded by handsome early automobiles. Courtesy of Key Bank

The Beacon side of the Newburgh-Beacon Ferry received a new terminal in 1915. It was photographed in this composite view taken at 3 P.M. on March 16, 1915. Courtesy of the Historical Society of Newburgh Bay and the Highlands

The ferry terminal on the Beacon side of the Hudson River shows the ferry approaching from Newburgh, at left. Courtesy of the Historical Society of Newburgh Bay and the Highlands

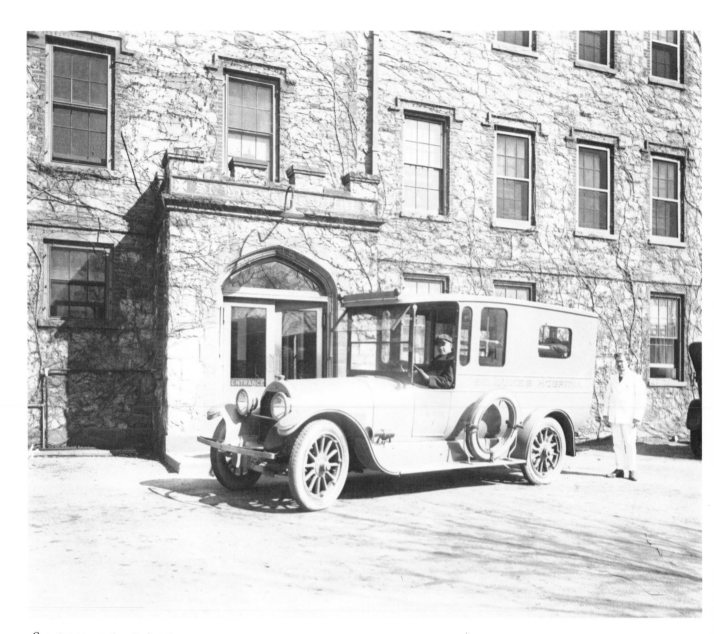

St. Luke's Hospital on Dubois Street in Newburgh began operations in a building that was originally the Associate Reformed Seminary. This undated photograph, signed by "Peck," shows one of the hospital's early ambulances. It was printed by the author from a glass plate negative in the collection of the historical society. Courtesy of the Historical Society of Newburgh Bay and the Highlands

A postcard shows an early view of St. Luke's Hospital in Newburgh, with four white-uniformed nurses standing out conspicuously against the dark background. Courtesy of Key Bank

The Newburgh Fire Department's pumper identified as C. M. Leonard No. 2 gleams in the sunlight in this undated photograph. Courtesy of the Historical Society of Newburgh Bay and the Highlands

A postcard view of the Newburgh (not Newburg!) Savings Bank looks eastward to the Hudson River and the distant mountains. Courtesy of Key Bank

A whimsical advertising card from one of Newburgh's early finance companies extols the virtues of borrowing to solve financial problems. Courtesy of the Historical Society of Newburgh Bay and the Highlands

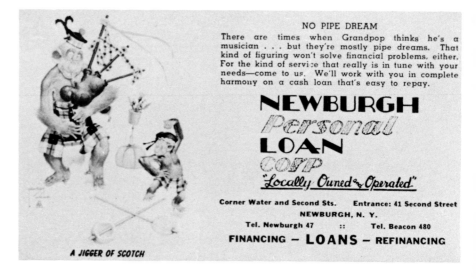

118

Clouds of smoke billow forth from a steam locomotive in the Erie Railroad yard in Newburgh, in this undated photograph. Courtesy of the Historical Society of Newburgh Bay and the Highlands

Two portraits show Annie Delano Hitch, for whom Newburgh's Delano Hitch Recreation Park is named. She was born about 1847 and died March 6, 1926. Her parents, Mr. and Mrs. Warren Delano, were residents of Balmville. Courtesy of the Historical Society of Newburgh Bay and the Highlands

The rink at Newburgh's Delano-Hitch Recreation Park was once an important national center for speed-skating competition, as suggested by this sponsor's certificate showing eighteen high-point winners for 1938. They are identified on the certificate as Charles Fullerton, Jack Lynch, Bryant Ormsby, Frank McKinstrie, John Thomas, Peter Farkas, Donald Jay, Robert Gilmore, Michael Moriello, John Farkas, William Dougherty, Jr., Bruce Baty, William O'Donnell, Campbell Hodge, Elmer Corwin, Thomas H. Stanton, Thomas Vincent, and Richard Palmer. Courtesy of the Historical Society of Newburgh Bay and the Highlands

"Historical Incidents" was the title of this costume pageant presented April 13, 1943, at the Dutch Reformed Church by the historical society. Courtesy of the Historical Society of Newburgh Bay and the Highlands

The durable overalls manufactured by Sweet-Orr & Co. in Newburgh were a nationally known brand of clothing. During World War II the so-called jungle suit (camouflage tones on one side, for jungle warfare, and muted tan on the reverse for desert wear) was developed at this plant, principally by production manager Albert B. Rhoades. Photo shows an unidentified Sweet-Orr employee in pressing room. Courtesy of the Historical Society of Newburgh Bay and the Highlands

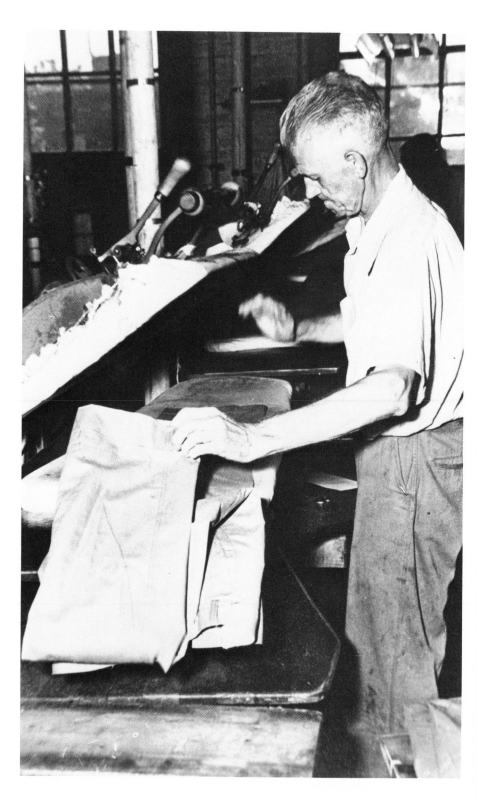

A Sweet-Orr display window and packing room were both photographed for Production for Freedom Week, September 6 to 13, 1952, sponsored by the Newburgh Chamber of Commerce. Sweet-Orr Plant No. 1 was at 274-284 Broadway; Plant No. 2 was at 327-329 Liberty Street. Courtesy of the Historical Society of Newburgh Bay and the Highlands

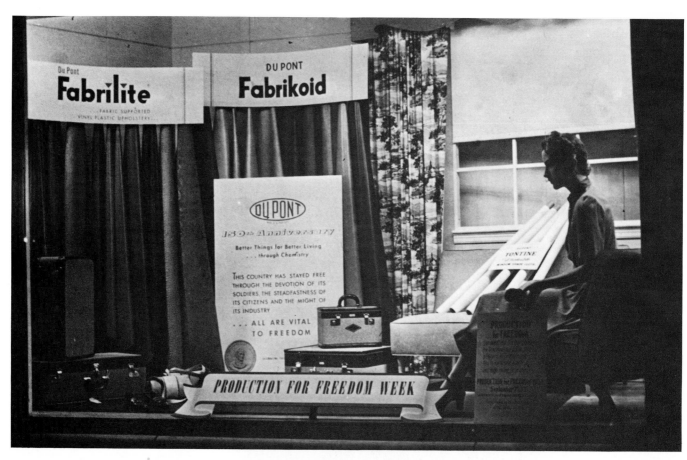

*E. I. DuPont de Nemours & Co., Inc. was
once one of Newburgh's principal employers,
at its former Fabrikoid plant complex on
Dupont Avenue, also known locally as the
Stauffer Chemical plant. This exhibit of
DuPont products was arranged for Production for Freedom Week, September 6 to 13,
1952, sponsored by the Newburgh Chamber
of Commerce. Courtesy of the Historical
Society of Newburgh Bay and the Highlands*

*Some eyesores near the city parking lot at the
rear of Ann and Washington streets came
under scrutiny during a Fire Prevention
effort on October 9, 1952. Photograph by Al
Rhoades, courtesy of the Historical Society of
Newburgh Bay and the Highlands*

Participants in a fire prevention presentation on October 11, 1952, included Benjamin Reed, Lt. Charles Whitehead, Thomas Kavanaugh, and R. Goodwin. Courtesy of the Historical Society of Newburgh Bay and the Highlands

Judging in a poster contest for Fire Prevention Week was held October 25, 1952. Included in the photograph are Calvin Myers, Frank Fletcher, Helen VerNooy Gearn, and LeGrand Pellet. Courtesy of the Historical Society of Newburgh Bay and the Highlands

The Newburgh Chamber of Commerce hosted a Regional Legislative Conference at the Palatine Hotel on October 17, 1952. Included in the photograph are (back row, from left) Homer Scace, J. Robert Markel, and Robert T. Eaton; (front row, from left) Edward G. O'Neill, William Mills, Edward Dillon, and Robert P. Aex. Courtesy of the Historical Society of Newburgh Bay and the Highlands

Col. Nelson Dingley, standing at the microphone, was the speaker at the Newburgh Chamber of Commerce annual dinner on October 29, 1952, in the Green Room of the Hotel Newburgh. Courtesy of the Historical Society of Newburgh Bay and the Highlands

A view of the speakers' table from the 1952 Chamber of Commerce annual dinner shows Ed Yates, chairman Bob Jamieson, and Ed O'Neill. Courtesy of the Historical Society of Newburgh Bay and the Highlands

Arthur D'Addazio presented a safety award to Diane Overbey on October 30, 1952. Courtesy of the Historical Society of Newburgh Bay and the Highlands

Peter Cantline was honored as Man of the Year for his community service, with Ed O'Neill presenting the award, at the Newburgh Chamber of Commerce Annual Dinner on October 29, 1952. Courtesy of the Historical Society of Newburgh Bay and the Highlands

A dramatic night photograph by Galati Studios shows South Water Street at the intersection of First Street on November 6, 1952. For the technically minded, Galati set his lens at f11 and exposed the SuperPan Press Type B film for twenty seconds. Photo by Galati Studios, courtesy of the Historical Society of Newburgh Bay and the Highlands

The Newburgh Chamber of Commerce Christmas Promotion Committee met for a preholiday planning session in 1952. Courtesy of the Historical Society of Newburgh Bay and the Highlands

Holiday caroling is still an annual tradition in Newburgh, just as it was when this photograph was taken on December 23, 1952, outside of 464 Broadway. Courtesy of the Historical Society of Newburgh Bay and the Highlands

Downtown Newburgh shimmers at night in these dramatic photographs from the 1950s by Galati Studios. Courtesy of the Historical Society of Newburgh Bay and the Highlands

Mayor Herbert Warden pulls the switch to light Newburgh's Yule lights for the 1952 holiday season. Courtesy of the Historical Society of Newburgh Bay and the Highlands

City Hall was in a bragging mood in January 1953 as Newburgh celebrated its designation as All-American City, selected for quality of local government. The photographer even captured a poster in a ground-floor window, warning: Water Meter Rents are Now Due. Photograph by Arthur L. Sigfried, courtesy of the Historical Society of Newburgh Bay and the Highlands

The Newburgh Chamber of Commerce hosted "All American Days" in February 1953. Courtesy of the Historical Society of Newburgh Bay and the Highlands

Judge Edward G. O'Neill is the speaker at this Newburgh Chamber of Commerce dinner on February 2, 1953. Courtesy of the Historical Society of Newburgh Bay and the Highlands

The Hudson River shows in the background of this photograph posed to promote Semi-annual Newburgh Days on April 15, 1953. The civic leaders at right are Hugh Whitehill Taylor and Tom Kavanaugh. Courtesy of the Historical Society of Newburgh Bay and the Highlands

Janet Brown was the appealing model who posed at the front bumper of a shiny Oldsmobile on April 28, 1953, to celebrate Newburgh's status as an "All-American City." Photograph by Al Rhoades, courtesy of the Historical Society of Newburgh Bay and the Highlands

A revealing shot of the contenders for Newburgh's Clean-Up Queen title was taken on May 11, 1953. Courtesy of the Historical Society of Newburgh Bay and the Highlands

In the days of vigorous downtown business promotion in Newburgh in 1953, shoppers were attracted by the prospect of winning a shiny new sedan. Courtesy of the Historical Society of Newburgh Bay and the Highlands

The car giveaway promotion acquired added allure when three local beauties posed with polishing cloths. Photograph by Al Rhoades, courtesy of the Historical Society of Newburgh Bay and the Highlands

Bathing beauties also helped to promote a cleaner Newburgh in this lineup of contestants for Miss Clean-Up. Personalities identified, from left, include Tom Kavanaugh, John Sloan White, Mayor Herbert Warden, Robert Hinsdale, Ed Yates, and Harry Cohen. Photograph by Vince Connolly, courtesy of the Historical Society of Newburgh Bay and the Highlands

Studying a map on August 28, 1953, are Newton Flemming, Ed Lloyd, Mayor Herbert Warden, and City Manager Robert Aex. Courtesy of the Historical Society of Newburgh Bay and the Highlands

Fire prevention was the topic of discussion at this gathering in Newburgh on September 12, 1953. Standing are Tom Kavanaugh, left, and Howard Flemming. Seated, from left, are R. H. Goodwin, John S. White and LeGrand Pellet. Courtesy of the Historical Society of Newburgh Bay and the Highlands

Eleanor Roosevelt visited Newburgh on October 19, 1953. She was introduced by Ed Yates, president of the Chamber of Commerce. Photograph by Al Rhoades, courtesy of the Historical Society of Newburgh Bay and the Highlands

The occasion for this photograph on February 27, 1954, was the American Bandmaster Concert held in Newburgh. Courtesy of the Historical Society of Newburgh Bay and the Highlands

Newburgh's Ed Yates poses with a uniformed representative of the American Bandmaster Association on February 27, 1954. Courtesy of the Historical Society of Newburgh Bay and the Highlands

Congresswoman Katherine B. St. George was photographed October 18, 1956, at a meeting of the Daughters of the American Revolution, Quassaick Chapter, on the occasion of her first visit to Crawford House after it had become the headquarters of the historical society. Photograph by Ruth Wilsey Valenti, courtesy of the Historical Society of Newburgh Bay and the Highlands

The Lily of France Company helped put Newburgh on the map as a maker of finest-quality ladies' unmentionables. The factory complex was on Route 17K, opposite Stewart Airport. Operators posed for this photograph on September 8, 1957. Courtesy of the Historical Society of Newburgh Bay and the Highlands

Developers and economic forecasters began to look at Newburgh with renewed respect and interest after the runaway success of builder Jim Salahshourian's Ferry Crossing Condominiums. The site on Water Street, long associated with Newburgh's history as a river town, lies between the former ferry slip at Second Street and the Newburgh-Beacon Bridge that replaced the ferry service. After decades of dormancy on the Newburgh riverfront, Salahshourian single-handedly re-populated the area by completing this luxury residential development in the first half of 1980. Photograph by Robert Paul Molay

The original north span of the
Newburgh-Beacon Bridge opened in 1963
and had developed its share of potholes in
eighteen years of continuous hard duty.
When the new south span was completed in
1981, the New York State Bridge Authority
shut down the north span for repairs. The
photograph shows the crew of John Arborio,
Inc., as they prepare on June 21, 1981 to
resurface and widen the bridge. At left are
mechanic Al Bahret and equipment operator
Ralph Chiumento; superintendent Thomas
Gumare is at right. Photograph by Robert
Paul Molay

Where once George Washington took his daily exercise, on Newburgh's Liberty Street, Mayor Joan Shapiro visits the Washington Market in 1983 for a chat with owner Eddie Rodriguez. Through an innovative "urban shopsteading" program and other initiatives, significant progress toward revitalizing Liberty Street was made during Mayor Shapiro's two terms in office, 1980 to 1987. Photograph by Robert Paul Molay

CHAPTER 4

A Glimpse at Orange County

West of the early Palatine settlement that became Newburgh, in the interior of Orange County, was the wilderness area known as the Wawayanda Patent. One of the patentees was Christopher Denn of Staten Island, the adoptive father of Sarah Wells.

To Orange County residents, Sarah Wells symbolizes the original pioneers who built in the wilderness. After hacking out a settlement in 1712 along the banks of the Otterkill Creek, in what is now the Town of Hamptonburgh, she married the stonemason William Bull. Their magnificent stone house was built in 1727 and is still in excellent condition except for the occasional nuisance of bats taking up residence in the upper story.

The Bull family has continued to play a prominent role in the public affairs of Orange County since the days of Sarah Wells. The most notable representative in our era is Amy Bull Crist, the educator.

In the consciousness of the nation and the world, Orange County is best known as the home of the United States Military Academy at West Point. The entire region around West Point was of crucial strategic importance during the Revolutionary War. Today, many residents of Newburgh and other parts of Orange County are part of the civilian employee force at West Point. The entire region benefits from West Point's drawing power as a tourist attraction for millions of visitors annually.

A modern view of cadets on parade on The Plain shows dress uniforms little changed from earlier days of the U.S. Military Academy. Photograph by Robert Paul Molay

The stone house erected in 1727 by skilled mason William Bull, still stands in a superlative state of preservation in the town of Hamptonburgh. Courtesy of the Historical Society of Newburgh Bay and the Highlands

Sarah Bull, affectionately known as Aunt Sally, was the daughter of Thomas Bull and granddaughter of Sarah Wells and William Bull. She was born in 1775 and lived until 1865. The photograph is signed "W. M. Knight, Buffalo, N.Y." Courtesy of Hill-Hold Museum

A photograph of the 1916 Bull family picnic and annual meeting is also in the collection of Hill-Hold. Courtesy of Hill-Hold Museum and the Orange County Department of Parks and Recreation

The Bull family is descended from Sarah Wells, the first European to settle permanently in the interior region of Orange County known as the Wawayanda Patent, and her husband, stonemason William Bull. The Bull family began the practice of holding annual meetings in 1821. Shown is a photograph of the 1919 meeting. Courtesy of Hill-Hold Museum

A committee organized in 1970 to restore the Bull family farm known as Hill-Hold included (back row, from left) Graham Skea, Orange County Commissioner of Parks and Recreation; Charles Peterson; Beatrice Rosenblum, antiques expert and columnist; Georgine Dunning; Brewster Board; Augustus Wallace; Peggy Prial; Amy Bull Crist, venerated educator and descendant of the Bull family; Werner Kaltenbach; Raymond Ruge, preservationist architect; Philip Sims, Orange County Parks Department; (kneeling, from left) Ruth Ottaway; Howard Armbruster; Eurnice Tenney; Robert Wiggins; and an unidentified young man in a bow tie. Courtesy of Hill-Hold Museum

Entrance to the Hudson Highlands was of such strategic importance during the Revolutionary War that the Continental Army stretched a massive iron chain across the river in 1776 in the vicinity of Fort Montgomery, intended to block the passage of British ships. The first chain—500 feet long and forged of 186 tons of iron—was broken October 7, 1777, by General John Vaughan, on his way to burn Kingston. The chain was replaced but never again tested by enemy forces. An original oil painting completed by Raymond L. Ciarcia, Fort Montgomery, in 1985 shows the area now spanned by the Bear Mountain Bridge. Photograph by Robert Paul Molay

A view of the Hudson River from Fort Putnam, now part of West Point, was published in London in 1837 by George Virtue, 26 Ivy Lane. Courtesy of the Historical Society of Newburgh Bay and the Highlands

The Corps of Cadets of the U.S. Military Academy at West Point parading on The Plain, in a nineteenth-century print that looks northward along the Hudson River into Newburgh Bay. Courtesy of Valice Ruge

Moffats Academy, as this fortresslike stone house was known from 1778 to 1781, made its contribution to the development of the Hudson Valley by providing instruction in Latin for both male and female students, including five children of General James Clinton: Alexander, Charles, George, DeWitt, and Mary. Construction was completed about 1745 by the Rev. John Little, who was related to the Clintons by marriage. Known today as Stonefield Farms, this view from 1981 shows the fine state of preservation of the former academy on Station Road in the Salisbury Mills section of New Windsor. Photograph by Robert Paul Molay

Chester National Bank was organized as a state bank in 1845, with original capital stock of $100,400, and received its charter as a national bank on June 6, 1865. The landmark stone building shown here (today housing the village of Chester Police Department) was constructed in 1895-1896.

William M. Bennett was the carpenter and roofer, and J. T. Thompson put in the plumbing. This pioneering institution, which bought its first adding machine in 1910, is now part of Key Bank. Photograph by Robert Paul Molay

John T. Johnson was the fifth president of Chester National Bank, one of the most vigorous and influential predecessors of the modern Key Bank. Johnson was born in Goshen in 1815. In his early twenties he was employed as a clerk to the contractor constructing the Illinois Central Railroad. Returning to Chester in 1843, he joined the mercantile establishment of his uncle, Francis Tuthill, who sat on the bank's first board of directors. Johnson was named cashier of the bank in 1851 and succeeded James Burt as bank president on June 10, 1881. He remained in this position until 1897, at which time Johnson was eighty-two years old. Photograph from Portrait and Biographical Record of Orange County, New York

A photograph taken shortly after dawn on April 18, 1983, shows the first train crossing the historic Moodna Viaduct in Mountainville, to inaugurate the new Metro-North commuter rail service from Port Jervis to Hoboken, New Jersey, on the west side of the Hudson River. Once part of the vast Erie-Lackawanna network that linked the Hudson with the Great Lakes, this towering trestle on the Graham Line was planned by J. M. Graham, the Erie's vice-president for engineering in the early twentieth century. Beneath the trestle runs the Moodna— originally Murderer's Creek because of an early Indian massacre. Photograph by Robert Paul Molay

Port Ewen, on the Hudson River just south of the Rondout, was also known as Sleightburgh. It was built by the Pennsylvania Coal Company to provide tidewater docking facilities. By 1865 the company ceased operations there and was shipping most of its coal to Newburgh via the Erie Railroad. This early photograph shows Hook & Ladder Company No. 1 of the Port Ewen Fire Department. Courtesy of the Historical Society of Newburgh Bay and the Highlands

CHAPTER 5

A Link to the Delaware

Coal was the energy source that propelled the railroad locomotives and Hudson River passenger liners in the great Age of Steam that extended well into the twentieth century. Coal also produced the iron and steel for American industry and even generated the electric power for later phases of industrial development.

If you have ever experimented with setting coal on fire, you know that it takes a considerable knack to make it burn. As late as the 1820s, the idea that coal could be used as a practical fuel was ridiculed by investors. Where there was an abundant supply of coal—on the Pennsylvania side of the Delaware River—there was no market for the product.

Maurice and William Wurts, businessmen of Philadelphia, conceived the idea of creating a waterway to transport Pennsylvania coal economically to New York City, where the potential market was enormous. "Canal fever" was in the air, as the Erie Canal was nearing completion and opened in 1825. Once the value of coal as fuel had been demonstrated, the Delaware and Hudson Canal Company was organized in 1825.

An intricate railroad system brought the coal from mines in the Carbondale vicinity to the beginning of the canal at Honesdale, Pennsylvania. It followed the course of the Delaware River to Port Jervis, where it made a right-angle turn to head northwest across Sullivan and Ulster counties to the tidewater of the Hudson River at Kingston.

The extensive lore of the D&H Canal is beyond the scope of this pictorial history devoted to the Mid-Hudson Valley. However, the growth, prosperity, and extensive commercial activity of Kingston in the nineteenth century cannot be explained without at least a brief mention of the canal.

The D&H opened officially in 1828. The first flotilla to navigate the entire 109-mile length departed from Rondout, now part of Kingston, on October 16, 1828, and the first squadron of coalboats from Honesdale, Pennsylvania, arrived at Rondout on December 5, 1828.

In its peak years of operation, in the 1870s, the D&H transported about two million tons of coal annually. The canal was almost single-handedly responsible for the birth of Port Jervis in the 1850s; in fact it was named for John B. Jervis, the chief engineer of the D&H.

Under competitive pressure from the railroads, the D&H ceased operations in 1898. The stagnant water in the canal became a hazard to public health and safety, and most of this once-renowned waterway was filled in long ago.

To the modern-day resident of the Mid-Hudson Valley, the Pennsylvania coal mines and the region of the Delaware River around Port Jervis seem so remote as to be almost in another world. During the seventy-year history of the D&H Canal, the Delaware and the Hudson were in a state of brisk, continuous communication.

Island Dock, officially known as Insular Dock, was completed in 1848 to add fourteen acres of shipping and receiving facilities for anthracite coal at the Rondout Docks of the Delaware & Hudson Canal Company.

Coal from Pennsylvania was here transferred to ships or barges capable of carrying the cargo down the Hudson River to markets along the Atlantic coast. In the early years, coal was unloaded on this manmade island

by swarms of laborers. When steam-powered coal elevators took over this task, labor troubles arose on the Rondout waterfront. Courtesy of Edwin M. Ford

SPEND YOUR VACATION IN

"THE MOST PICTURESQUE MOUNTAIN
REGION ON THE GLOBE,"

THE CATSKILL MOUNTAINS.

"Like mighty thinkers, there they stand
Above the soft, green pasture land;
Those grand, calm heights, like sages, hold
Such treasures heaped from times of old;
Unquenched the living waters flow
Which verdure brings to fields below."

THE ONLY STANDARD GAUGE LINE AND
THROUGH CAR SERVICE TO THIS FAMOUS
AND HEALTHFUL MOUNTAIN REGION IS VIA

The Ulster & Delaware Railroad.

SEND EIGHT CENTS POSTAGE FOR ILLUSTRATED SUMMER BOOK,
WITH MAP OF THE CATSKILLS AND COMPLETE LIST OF HOTELS
AND BOARDING HOUSES.

N. A. SIMS, General Passenger Agent, Rondout, N. Y.

Ulster & Delaware Railroad was operating as early as May 1870, under the Roundout & Oswego name, with connections from Rondout to the Catskill Mountain vacationlands and a route to market in New York City for milk produced on farms in the Catskills. In the 1890s, Samuel Decker Coykendall conceived the plan for remodeling the Delaware & Hudson Canal wharf at Kingston Point, to be joined there by the Ulster & Delaware Railroad. After 1896 the Hudson River Day Line steamers abandoned calling at Rhinecliff, on the east bank of the Hudson River, and began offering passengers a direct rail connection at Kingston Point Park. This advertisement, billing the Catskills as "The Haunts of Rip Van Winkle," appeared in 1900. Courtesy of Alfred P. Marquart

This view of the docks at Rondout was taken to highlight the loading machinery manufactured by American Hoist & Derrick Co. of St. Paul, Minnesota. Courtesy of Alfred P. Marquart

157

New York State's first senate house, built around 1676, is possibly the oldest public building in the United States. Standing on Clinton Avenue near the corner of North Front Street in Kingston, it was built as a private residence by Col. Wessel Ten Broeck. The house was thus more than a century old when the state constitution was adopted there on April 20, 1777. After the city was torched by the British on October 16, 1777, the sturdy stone walls of the Senate House and many other old stone houses were found to have survived the conflagration. This view of the Senate House taken about 1900 looks southward on Clinton Avenue toward Main Street, with Clinton Avenue still unpaved more than two hundred years after the days of Colonel Ten Broeck. Courtesy of Edwin M. Ford

CHAPTER 6

Kingston

Modern Kingston combines several communities named in a variety of languages reflecting the Dutch, English, and Indian influences of earlier days.

At the time of Henry Hudson's visit, there was a settlement of Esopus or Waynawanck Indians at the juncture of the creek now called the Rondout with the river now called the Hudson. In addition to the widely used names for the river mentioned in Chapter One, it was also called *Cahohatatia* in Algonquin, *Mahkeneghtue* in Mohegan, and *Skanektade* by various other tribes.

The Esopus residents called their settlement *Atharkarton*, meaning "lovely land" in their language. Henry Hudson is believed to have reached this settlement on September 12, 1609, obtaining a supply of fresh water from the Rondout.

Although there is some evidence of a Dutch trading post at the mouth of the Rondout in 1610, there was definitely an establishment of the Dutch East India Company at this site by 1614. Little is known about the trading post at Kingston Point, but the one called *Punthoekje* in Dutch has been remembered in the corrupt form of *Ponckhockie* and many variant spellings.

The first permanent-settlement, and the date from which Kingston reckons its important anniversaries, arose from a deed for land obtained by Thomas Chambers on June 5, 1652. As the relations with the Indians grew more hostile, Governor Peter Stuyvesant chose a site for a stockade, completed on June 21, 1658.

The settlement within the stockade was known as Esopus until 1661, when it was changed to Wiltwyck. An earlier fort or redoubt—*ronduit* in Dutch—had been built by the other group of Dutch traders near Kingston Point. The name Rondout has ever since applied both to the creek that meets the Hudson there and the community on its banks. Some sources say the Indian name for the Rondout was *Thopackock*.

After a series of bloody wars with the Esopus Indians, the Dutch settlement came under English rule on September 8, 1664, as a proprietary colony of the duke of York. The name Kingston was first used in 1669. Yet one more name change awaited Kingston in 1673, when the Dutch regained their rule for the brief period of fifteen months and named it Swanenburg. From 1685 until the Revolutionary War Kingston was part of the royal colony of New York.

Kingston was the first capital of New York State. Perhaps as punishment for its role in framing the first New York State Constitution and accommodating the inaugural state legislature, Kingston was burned by the British on October 16, 1777.

Kingston and Rondout were incorporated into the city of Kingston in 1872.

Kingston's justifiable pride in its long and glorious past, its important role in early settlement of the Hudson Valley, the War for Independence and the birth of New York State, were all manifested in the three-hundredth anniversary celebration which opened December 30, 1951. Henry Hudson had stopped in the Kingston vicinity on September 12, 1609, to draw drinking water from the Rondout Creek for the crew of the Half Moon, *and traders from the Dutch East India Company had already entered into commerce with the Indians at Atharkarton (near the mouth of the Rondout) by 1614. But Kingston chose 1652, the date of Thomas Chambers' treaty with the Indians granting him seventy-six acres along the Esopus Creek, as the first definite date in its development as a community. Shown here is a souvenir booklet from the tercentenary celebration. Courtesy of Alfred P. Marquart*

Another view of the Senate House in Kingston, taken in winter, shows more structural details of this oldest building owned by the state of New York. The state's first senate convened there in 1777, probably in the large room at the far (south) end of the house. This room had a separate entrance, marked by a tablet over the door that is visible in the photograph as a white rectangle. Other parts of the house were occupied during the Revolutionary War era by Abraham Van Gaasbeek. The rear wall of this venerable stone house is built of brick, a feature common to many seventeenth-century houses in Ulster County. The photograph has been published, without credits, in at least four histories of Kingston.

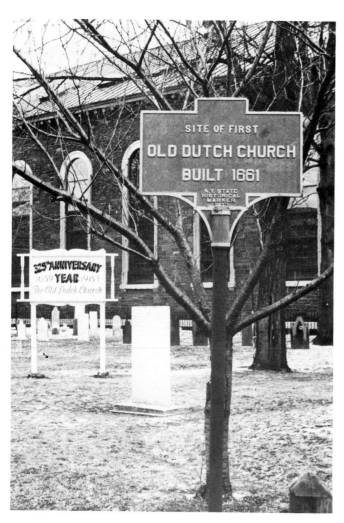

Early Dutch settlers of Wiltwyck—as Peter Stuyvesant named the forerunner of Kingston—met for worship in private houses, listening to bible readings by the voorleezer, Adrien Van der Sluys. The first Dutch Reformed Church was built of wood in 1661. After a few years it was replaced by a larger stone edifice, which was remodeled in 1721, rebuilt and enlarged in 1752, burned by the British in 1777 and completely reconstructed by 1790. It was razed in 1830 to make way for the fourth building in the line of succession of the Old Dutch Church, a brick structure on the northeast corner of Wall and Main streets completed August 20, 1833. This photograph taken in 1981, shows tombstones of old Kingston settlers, with the present (1852) Dutch Reformed Church in the background. Photograph by Robert Paul Molay

A good overall view of Kingston's Old Dutch Reformed Church is shown in this postcard. Courtesy of Alfred P. Marquart

The Dutch Reformed Church, perhaps Kingston's best known landmark, was completed and dedicated on September 28, 1852, on a site that had been used for religious worship for almost two hundred years. The site is bounded by Wall, Fair and Main streets. A tornado toppled the steeple on December 24, 1853, damaging the church and closing it for repairs until May 8, 1854. The photograph shows the steeple once again undergoing repairs (note workman suspended near the top, at left) on May 26, 1966. Photograph by John M. Kruli, in collection of Harry Rigby, Jr., courtesy of Edwin M. Ford

Key Bank in Kingston traces its origins to 1836, when the original Kingston Bank was chartered. In 1839 Kingston Bank began conducting its business in this building at Main and Ford streets, once considered the most impressive banking house in the city. After the Civil War it was known as Kingston National Bank and in 1920, it received a state charter as Kingston Trust Company. Photograph by Henry Ziegler, courtesy of Key Bank

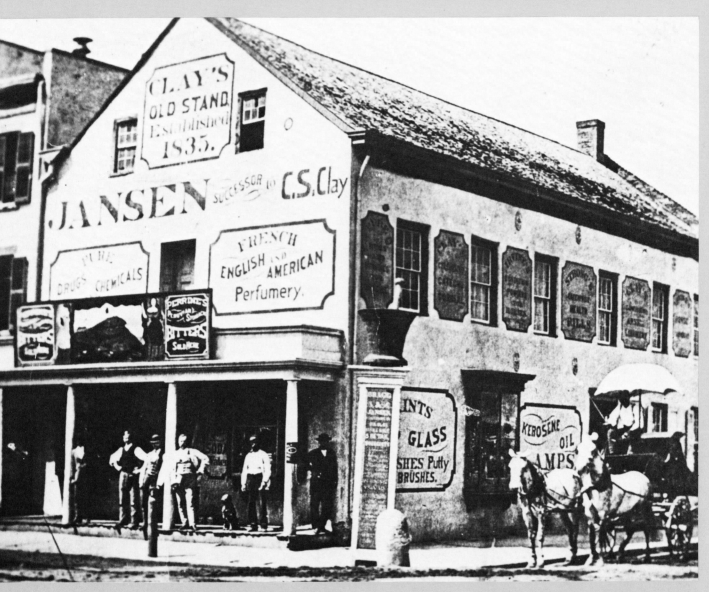

Caleb S. Clay opened shop in Kingston in 1835 in the corner building at 1 Wall Street and 67 North Front Street. The Kingston & Rondout Directory 1857-8 lists Clay as treasurer of the village of Kingston and a resident of Hurley Avenue, Mapleton. An advertisement in the same directory reads: "C. S. Clay, wholesale and retail dealer in drugs, medicines, chemicals, paints, oils, dye stuffs, window glass, &c," and reveals that Clay was also operator of the Ulster County Life & Fire Insurance Agency. By 1870, the date of this photograph, Peter E. Jansen had taken over Clay's drugstore. Courtesy of Edwin M. Ford

Wall Street in Kingston, viewed from North Front Street, shows this busy thoroughfare as it appeared in 1870, with horses drawing a cart on tracks at right. Next to Jansen's Drugstore at right is James O. Merritt & Company; at left are Sanler & Reynolds Hardware Store and Van Deusen Brothers Groceries. Courtesy of Edwin M. Ford

The Kingston City Home, shown here in a postcard view, was at first known as the Poor House. It was built on Flatbush Avenue in 1872-73, under the leadership of Mayor James G. Lindsley and the newly organized Board of Alms Commissioners. To combat the unemployment of the day, workmen who built the home were paid food and clothing plus fifty cents a day for their labor. Courtesy of Alfred P. Marquart

Before there could be a Kingston City Hall, there had to be a city—a consideration that was almost decided in favor of Rondout. Rondout, growing rapidly by 1871, applied to the state legislature for a city charter, but Kingston's nascent civic pride won the day. Rondout was incorporated into the new city of Kingston in 1872. City Hall was erected in 1873 at 408 Broadway (formerly the Strand), midway between the former villages of Rondout and Kingston. It was built of Philadelphia pressed brick, with stone trimmings, at a cost of seventy-five thousand dollars. The photograph shows City Hall as it was built, prior to the fire of 1927 that necessitated extensive rebuilding. Collection of Harry Rigby Jr., courtesy of Edwin M. Ford

S. *and W. B. Fitch, dealers in North River bluestone, used the building at far left as their main office on the banks of the Rondout. Sailing vessels in the background are sloops and schooners of the Fitch Line, used to transport the Catskill Mountain bluestone down the Hudson (or North River) to New York City for use as sidewalks. The illustration, originally in* Ulster County Atlas of 1875, *was reprinted in the* Kingston Tercentenary Souvenir Booklet. *Courtesy of Alfred P. Marquart*

*K*ingston *turned out in force to accord a hearty civic greeting when the circus came to town, as shown in this photograph taken about 1880, looking north on Wall Street from the Ulster Savings Bank building. Courtesy of Edwin M. Ford*

The cornerstone of Kingston City Hospital was laid on April 22, 1893, and the hospital was formally opened on November 27, 1894. Courtesy of Alfred P. Marquart

Another postcard view of Kingston City Hospital, which was kept busy in its earliest days treating victims of industrial accidents arising from cement quarrying, the railroads, and the sunset days of the D&H Canal. Courtesy of Alfred P. Marquart

169

Rodney A. Chipp, Edward Jung, Geo. Wachmeyer, Jr., Chas. A. Mills.

Hubert Rush, C. L. Quackenbush, William Heybruck.

Kingston hosted the twelfth annual Hudson Valley Volunteer Firemen's Association convention and tournament, June 18-19, 1901. The fire department of the city of Kingston traces its origins to November 27, 1754, when the Corporation of Kingston instructed Trustee Petrus E. Elmendorf to order a fire engine from England. This engine, delivered in 1757, rendered good service until it was destroyed in the fire of 1777 set by Gen. John Vaughan and his sixteen hundred British troops. Shown in the official program of the convention were officers of the city fire department in 1901: (top row, from left) Rodney A. Chipp, first assistant chief; Edward Jung, fourth assistant chief; George Wachmeyer, Jr., treasurer; Charles A. Mills, assistant secretary; (bottom row, from left) Hubert Rush, second assistant chief; Charles Layton Quackenbush, chief engineer; and William Heybruck, third assistant engineer. Courtesy of Alfred P. Marquart

Isaac N. Weiner was a charter member of Kingston's Franklin Hose Company No. 6, organized April 12, 1878. So active in the company affairs were Isaac and Richard Weiner that the name was soon changed to Ike and Dick Hose Company No. 6. On Oct. 9, 1885, it became more formally known as the Weiner Hose Company. Its engine house on Hasbrouck Avenue, directly to the rear of City Hall, was conveniently near to Weiner's liquor store. Perhaps for this reason the Hudson Valley Volunteer Firemen's Association was moved to comment, in 1900: "As entertainers the members (of Weiner Hose) have few equals." The advertisement shown here is from the official program of the firemen's convention. Courtesy of Alfred P. Marquart

Dutch dominance of Kingston's cultural life had relaxed enough by 1900, apparently, to create a local market for German-style beer. An advertisment for Peter Barmann's Thuringer Hofbrau appeared in the official program of the Hudson Valley Volunteer Firemen's Association convention for 1901. Courtesy of Alfred P. Marquart

With the trolley line of the Kingston Consolidated Railroad terminating at water's edge at Kingston Point, some accidents were to be expected. These two postcards appear to show different views of the same accident that occurred in the early part of 1901. Courtesy of Alfred P. Marquart

172

Cordts Hose Company No. 8, a unit of the Kingston Fire Department, was organized in February 1894 by John N. Cordts. Officers of the company in 1901 were Mr. Cordts, president; James Kelly, foreman; Alexander Brown, first assistant foreman; Henry Grenke, second assistant foreman; James C. Penny, secretary; William H. Penny, treasurer; Thomas Hart, janitor; and George Adams and Peter Lemister, trustees. Company members in this undated photograph have not been identified. Courtesy of Alfred P. Marquart

Peter Stuyvesant ordered construction of the stockade at Wiltwyck, the Dutch settlement that later became Kingston, on May 30, 1658. A rare photograph by F. C. Wells shows Kingston's latter-day citizens—surely dressed in red, white, and blue—marking the 250th anniversary of the stockade on May 30, 1908. Courtesy of Alfred P. Marquart

George Clinton, the first governor of New York State and twice elected vice-president of the United States, was originally buried in the Congressional Cemetery in Washington when he died in 1812. His remains were transferred to Kingston in 1908 and he is now interred to the west of the main entrance into the Old Dutch Church yard. The monument marking his grave was erected by the Daughters of the American Revolution. Photo by Lane Studios, courtesy of Edwin M. Ford

*As many as ten thousand people a day
visited Kingston Point Park in 1903, shown
here in a postcard view. In mid-1987 the
Kingston Recreation Department began
planning seriously to clean up and infuse
new life into the old park site. Courtesy of
Alfred P. Marquart*

In its peak years of the early twentieth century, Kingston Point Park became a fairyland of wholesome amusements for warm-weather visitors. It was a particular favorite of Sunday school groups, who often chartered river steamers for the trip to Kingston from distant cities. This postcard was mailed in 1908. Courtesy of Alfred P. Marquart

This view of the trolley-line terminal at Kingston Point Park is from a postcard mailed in 1908. Courtesy of Alfred P. Marquart

Riverside *was the proper name of the chain ferry between Rondout and Port Ewen, shown in a view from a postcard post-marked in 1912. Behind the group of men to the right, and at their left, are loaded wagons. When Kingston entered the auto-mobile age, the* Riverside *could just barely accommodate four automobiles. Courtesy of Alfred P. Marquart*

Prior to 1921, when a two-lane highway suspension bridge was completed between Rondout and Port Ewen, the Skillipot chain ferry provided transportation across the creek. Rondout lost its separate political identity when it was incorporated into the city of Kingston in 1872, and Sleightburgh (often spelled Sleightsburgh) was an early name for Port Ewen. The Skillipot was propelled by a steel chain running across the bed of the Rondout, securely fastened to the dock at either side. A steam engine turned a large steel drum to wind and unwind the chain. Photograph in the Harry Rigby, Jr., Collection, courtesy of Edwin M. Ford

THE KINGSTON
AND
SLEIGHTBURGH FERRY CO.

2c   J. Hasbrouck
     Pres.

88182

THE KINGSTON
AND
SLEIGHTBURGH FERRY CO.

15c   J. Hasbrouck
      Pres.

14676

The former Kingston Post Office, as shown in an old postcard. Courtesy of Alfred P. Marquart

A postcard mailed in 1914 shows Kingston's Stuyvesant Hotel, named after Peter Stuyvesant, first Dutch governor of the colony that eventually became New York State. Courtesy of Alfred P. Marquart

Among the interesting details in this postcard view of the West Shore and Union Station in Kingston is the workman in right foreground, dressed in suit and bowler hat, leaning on a shovel. Courtesy of Alfred P. Marquart

A bird's-eye view of Kingston is from a postcard published by the Kingston Souvenir Company, bearing a 1914 postmark. Courtesy of Alfred P. Marquart

Kingston School No. 4 was known earlier in its career as Ponckhockie Union School or Free School, with students of high school age. When Kingston High School opened on September 6, 1915, School No. 4 became a grade school. Courtesy of Alfred P. Marquart

Among Kingston's contributions to the national effort in World War I was this all-female unit of the Ambulance Motor Corps, Home Defense Reserves. The year was 1918, as can be confirmed from the date on the license plate of the ambulance. The photograph was printed in the Kingston Tercentenary Souvenir Booklet (1652-1952). Courtesy of Alfred P. Marquart

Members of the Home Guard, World War I, posed in front of the old Kingston Armory on Broadway. The photograph is from the Kingston Tercentenary Souvenir Booklet. Courtesy of Alfred P. Marquart

Another old parade scene shows a spirited line of marchers passing the former Kingston Post Office bedecked in patriotic bunting. The occasion and the date were not recorded. Courtesy of Alfred P. Marquart

KINGSTON TRUST CO.

Main Office—Corner Main and Fair Streets

Central Branch—518 Broadway

Kingston, New York

Total Resources $16,000,000. Capital Surplus and Undivided Profits $1,669,000.00. The Kingston Bank was organized in 1865. Changed its name to Kingston National Bank in 1865 and on May 19, 1919 became Kingston Trust Co. Main office is located in original building corner Main and Fair Streets.

Central Branch of Kingston Trust Co. was opened at 518 Broadway March 20, 1920. This 300th anniversary of the City of Kingston finds the Kingston Trust Co. also celebrating its success by rebuilding and enlarging its central branch quarters to the effect shown above. The growth of Kingston Trust Co. places it within the first 1300 of all the banks in the United States of which there are more than 14,000. In addition to conducting a general banking business, commercial checking and interest bearing accouts, loans and discounts, Christmas clubs and safe deposit boxes, a trust department acts as executor, administrator and trustee of estates of individuals, trustee under voluntary or irrevocable trusts, custodian of real or personal property, guardian of estates of minors and committee of estates of incompetents.

The affairs of Kingston Trust Co. are governed by the following directors: Holley R. Cantine, Martine Cantine Co.; Adelbert H. Chambers, Stuyvesant Motors, Maple Lane Farms; Arthur A. Davis, Vice President and Treasurer; Bernard A. Feeney, Marine Transportation; Stephen D. Hiltebrant, C. Hiltebrant Dry Dock Co.; Joseph E. Honig, Max Ulman, Inc., County Club Frocks, Inc.; Arthur V. Hornbeek, Ellenville, N. Y.; George F. Kaufman, attorney; Ernest LeFevre, Vice President and Assistant Treasurer; George Rusk, attorney; Fabian L. Russell, F. L. Russell Corp.; Alva S. Staples, President, Brick Manufacture; Cornelius S. Treadwell, Kingston, N. Y.; David Terry, Kingston, N. Y.; Henry J. Wieber, Wieber and Walter, Inc.

The affairs of Kingston Trust Co. are under the immediate supervision of the following officers: Alva S. Staples, President; Arthur A. Davis, Vice President and Treasurer; Ernest LeFevre, Vice President and Assistant Treasurer; Gordon A. Craig, Secretary and Assistant Treasurer; Frank Finley, Assistant Treasurer; Vernon S. Miller, Assistant Treasurer; William Muchem, Assistant Treasurer; George C. Bode, Assistant Treasurer; Ellis H. Griffith, Trust Officer; George F. Kaufman, Counsel.

Member of Federal Reserve Bank of New York. Federal Deposit Insurance Corp. American Bankers Association. New York State Bankers Association. New York State Safe Deposit Association.

An intermediate stage in the history of Key Bank in Kingston was the opening of the Central Branch of Kingston Trust Company on March 20, 1920. An advertisement from 1952 shows a contemporary view of the Central Branch at 518 Broadway, as it was rebuilt and enlarged at the time of the Kingston Tercentenary Celebration. Courtesy of Alfred P. Marquart

The Governor Clinton Hotel on Albany Avenue, opposite Academy Green, opened for occupancy on May 15, 1926. Its advertising stated: "Situated at the Foot Hills of the Catskill and Shawangunk Mountains. In the beautiful City of Kingston. Modern in every detail." Courtesy of Alfred P. Marquart

Railroad tracks crossed Kingston's Broadway at grade level, giving rise to frequent accidents, until 1952, when the crossing was eliminated. Courtesy of Alfred P. Marquart

187

The legend under this work reads: "A View in Hudson's River of Pakepsey & the Catt's-Kill Mountains, from Sopos Island in Hudson's River, Sketch'd on the Spot by his Excellency Governor Pownal, Painted & Engraved by Paul Sandby." Courtesy of Valice Ruge

CHAPTER 7

Poughkeepsie: A Case Study in Valuing the Past

Poughkeepsie's three-hundredth birthday, celebrated in 1987, makes this city on the east bank of the Hudson River a few decades younger than Kingston and a few decades older than Newburgh.

Like her sister cities in the Mid-Hudson Valley, Poughkeepsie was showing her age in the 1960s and 1970s. The steamer service had been abandoned, the annual crew racing regatta had moved elsewhere, and businesses were escaping from the lower section of Main Street near the river.

Poughkeepsie had its responsible municipal government to ponder the rights and wrongs of urban renewal, and to plan a productive future for the neglected assets of this river city. However, it is not the government effort that will be discussed here, but rather the effort that arose from private citizens, to preserve one of Poughkeepsie's most glorious memories of her nineteenth-century past.

As a weekend visitor to Poughkeepsie in 1967, I went to the Bardavon movie theater at 35 Market Street to see The Beatles' *Yellow Submarine.* In the dim interior light, I could see nothing to distinguish this movie palace from hundreds of others—except perhaps that the upholstery on the seats was a little dingy and that some of the decor looked vaguely "classical."

A decade later, everyone in Poughkeepsie was paying attention to the Bardavon because its new owners had applied to the city manager for permission to demolish it. The intended use of the valuable land on Market Street was to create a parking lot for the adjacent Poughkeepsie Savings Bank.

Stephen W. Dunwell and his wife, Julia, were two Poughkeepsie residents who understood that the Bardavon was more than just a characterless movie house. They formed the nucleus of a citizens' group that determined to save the Bardavon.

Before it could be saved, its value had to be appreciated. Research showed that the Bardavon was actually a full-fledged opera house, built by prosperous coal merchant James Collingwood in 1869. Collingwood had traveled to the great concert halls of Europe to collect ideas for his opera house, and the best materials were lavished on its construction. Although superlative acoustics cannot always be planned, Collingwood's calculations worked, because the unamplified sound quality in his opera house is rich, warm and balanced.

The roof line had been altered after 1869 to create a five-story flyloft above the stage, making it possible to change scenes rapidly with elaborately painted backdrops "flown" from ropes and pulleys in the loft. Some inquiries showed that the Bardavon was New York State's only remaining proscenium-arch theater between New York and Albany. Its ropes, pulleys and sandbags made it one of the very few "hemp" houses still functioning in the theater world.

All the great personalities of the late nineteenth and early twentieth centuries had played in Poughkeepsie. Mme. Ernestine Schumann-Heinck used to arrive by steamer at the foot of Main Street with three wagonloads of trunks to see her through her singing engagements. The Bardavon stage was graced by Caruso, Sarah Bernhardt, Paderewski, John Philip

Sousa. It was George M. Cohan's favorite theater for out-of-town trials of new Broadway musicals.

Even though this distinguished past had been forgotten for a few decades, underneath its degraded status as a movie house the Bardavon was still usable as a concert hall and theater. It took the imminent approach of the wrecker's ball to wake up Poughkeepsie to its potential for another chapter of useful life.

Suddenly, the Dunwells and their circle of tireless volunteers had switched on the spotlights and footlights and there was new life in the Bardavon. By the fall of 1978 there was real opera on the stage of the Bardavon, with a full contingent of musicians from the Hudson Valley Philharmonic in the orchestra pit.

Then there was help from the Poughkeepsie Urban Renewal Agency, the New York State Council on the Arts, the National Endowment for the Arts, the New York State Department of Parks and Recreation, and thousands of private contributors and volunteers. Even the Poughkeepsie Savings Bank, which had fought to keep a parking lot from being snatched from its grasp, eventually became a supporter of the Bardavon. As the sign on the marquee proclaimed on the day the Bardavon 1869 Opera House, Inc., took title to the venerable theater building: "You did it, Poughkeepsie!"

Matthew Vassar of Poughkeepsie spent $685,000—half the fortune he had amassed as a brewer of ale—to endow a women's college in 1861. Today this college in Arlington is one of the most prestigious in the world, and its endowment has grown to over $200 million. Vassar now has an enrollment of twenty-three hundred, and a thousand employees with a payroll of $20.5 million annually. It became coeducational in 1969. The photograph shows the Lodge, the main entrance to the Vassar campus on Raymond Avenue, Poughkeepsie, as it appeared about 1900. Courtesy of Alfred P. Marquart

190

The sacrifices made by Poughkeepsie's fighting men in the Civil War are remembered in this local landmark, the Soldier's Fountain, shown as it appeared in 1980. It is dramatically illuminated at night during the warm seasons. Photograph by Robert Paul Molay

The railroad bridge between Poughkeepsie and Highland, once dubbed the Ninth Wonder of the World, was begun on November 14, 1876. Its original purpose was to provide a link for the Poughkeepsie and Eastern Railroad betweeen the coal fields of Pennsylvania and the coal-consuming industries of New England. The project was delayed for years by a construction accident that drove the American Bridge Company into bankruptcy. The first train crossed the bridge on December 29, 1888, and the first passenger train two days later. The railroad bridge has been out of service since a fire in 1974. Its half mile of track, at an elevation of 212 feet above the Hudson River, was purchased for one dollar in 1984 by Gordon Schreiber Miller. Courtesy of Alfred P. Marquart

The Bardavon Office Building at 35 Market Street in Poughkeepsie shields the front of the Opera House from sight. This 1981 view from the rear shows the roof line as originally constructed in 1869, plus the addition (in lighter-colored brick) that brought the flyloft up to a full five stories' height. Despite its superlative acoustics and distinguished history, the Bardavon came within a hair's breadth of demolition to make way for a parking lot in 1978. Photograph by Robert Paul Molay

The proscenium arch construction of the Bardavon 1869 Opera House, shown in 1980, makes it one of the few remaining theaters in the Hudson Valley where full-size "flown" backdrops can be changed rapidly by means of ropes and pulleys extending far above the visible portion of the stage. Photograph by Robert Paul Molay

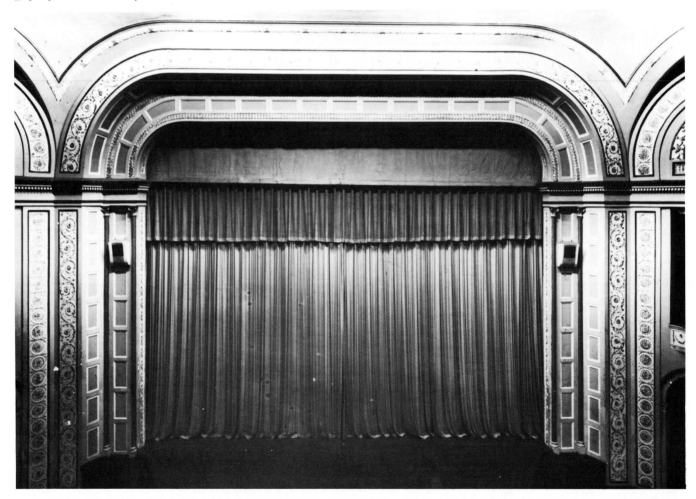

As originally built by James Collingwood, the Opera House in Poughkeepsie had no marquee. This picture from an old newspaper clipping shows the marquee as it appeared in the 1920s. Courtesy of Julia Dunwell

Full-scale productions of live opera returned to the stage (and the orchestra pit) of the Bardavon 1869 Opera House in September 1978, crowning the efforts of a citizens' group that saved the building from demolition and established it as a regional performing arts center. Photograph by Robert Paul Molay

The big day in the Bardavon drama came on April 25, 1979, when the Bardavon 1869 Opera House, Inc., formally took title to the building—permanently ending the threat of demolition. Prior to ceremonies in the theater, there was a parade down the Main Mall in Poughkeepsie, and some outdoor orations. Stephen W. Dunwell, left, was the first chairman of the board of directors of the nonprofit citizens' group that steered the preservation project through its initial rough days. At right is the Hon. John T. "Jack" Kennedy, mayor of Poughkeepsie in this era. Photograph by Robert Paul Molay

The theme of the big parade and other festivities on April 25, 1979—the day the future of the Bardavon became secure—was "You Did It Poughkeepsie!" The cherubic face at left is the author's son, Joshua. Photograph by Robert Paul Molay

ACQUISITION OF THE BARDAVON 1869 OPERA HOUSE
Project Name: COLLINGWOOD OPERA HOUSE

...which is listed on the National Register of Historic Places, has been partially funded with grants from:

· HERITAGE CONSERVATION AND RECREATION SERVICE
· NEW YORK STATE OFFICE OF PARKS AND RECREATION DIVISION FOR HISTORIC PRESERVATION

Hugh L. Carey, GOVERNOR
Orin Lehman, STATE HISTORIC PRESERVATION OFFICER

and
CITY OF POUGHKEEPSIE COMMUNITY DEVELOPMENT
with funds from the U.S.D.H.U.D.

John T. Kennedy, MAYOR

A temporary sign in the theater lobby, posted in 1979, evidenced the fact that the original effort to save the Opera House by a group of private citizens had gathered momentum, and was now supported by state and local government. Photograph by Robert Paul Molay

A view of Poughkeepsie at twilight, taken in 1980 from Highland, shows the Mid-Hudson Bridge, which was built in the late 1920s at a cost of $6 million. Photograph by Robert Paul Molay

Aerial photograph of lower Broadway and the Newburgh riverfront shows the corporate headquarters building of Key Bank as it nears completion. Courtesy of Key Bank; photographs by Santacroce Studio

CHAPTER 8

The Future

All along the Mid-Hudson Valley, as recently as 1980, there were stretches of wasteland, extensive parcels of riverfront property that had been abandoned to vandalism and the elements. Newburgh's Water Street, the center of commercial life for more than a century, had become a ghost town with real-life desperadoes.

These properties entered into their period of decline because they had been linked to the technologies of an outmoded age—the heavy industries and the supremacy of the river steamers and the railroads.

Since 1980, the riverfront in the Mid-Hudson Valley has been returning to productivity. The river view and the beauty of the changing seasons along the Hudson make it extremely attractive for housing development. Those who have risked investing in this concept—such as the Ferry Crossing Condominiums in Newburgh—have been highly successful. In keeping with this trend, much of Newburgh's once-industrial river frontage is currently in the process of becoming residential neighborhoods.

White-collar service industries are supplanting the smoke-belching mills and forges of an earlier age. The corporate headquarters of Key Bank, on a high vantage point overlooking the Hudson at the foot of Broadway in Newburgh, is being completed just as this book goes into publication.

The Indians that Henry Hudson observed will never dance again by moonlight at Danskammer—they would be chased away by the Central Hudson security guards. The New England whaling vessels will not call again at Newburgh, Poughkeepsie, and Kingston. The *Alexander Hamilton* has taken her last voyage on the river.

But all the signs indicate that the leaders and residents of the Mid-Hudson Valley are taking better care of their river and its banks than they did in the middle decades of this century.

It is hoped that this book, by awakening memories of our rich historical heritage, will stimulate the desire to use the precious riverfront wisely in the age of rapid development that is now approaching.

Bibliography

Carmer, Carl. *The Hudson*. New York: Farrar & Rinehart, 1939.

———. *Portrait and Biographical Record of Orange County, New York*. New York and Chicago: Chapman Publishing Co., 1895.

Decker & Fowler, Inc. *Old Kingston Illustrated*. Kingston, N.Y.: Freeman Publishing Co., 1923.

DeLisser, Richard Lionel. *Picturesque Ulster*. Kingston, N.Y.: The Styles & Bruyn Publishing Company, 1896. Reprint. Woodstock, N.Y.: Privately printed, 1968.

Eager, Samuel M., Esq. *An Outline History of Orange County*. 1846-1847. Reprint. Middletown, N.Y.: T. Emmett Henderson, 1971.

Forman, Sidney. *The American Revolution in the Hudson Highlands*. Cornwall, N.Y.: The News of the Highlands, Inc., 1982.

Fowler, Everett. *The Founding and Early Development of Kingston, New York*. Kingston; Privately printed, 1924.

Hickey, Andrew S. *The Story of Kingston, First Capital of New York State*. New York: Stratford House, 1952.

Lossing, Benson J. *The Hudson, From the Wilderness to the Sea*. Troy, N.Y.: H. B. Nims & Co., 1866.

Mailler, Marion M., and Dempsey, Janet. *Eighteenth Century Homes in New Windsor and its Vicinity*. New Windsor, N.Y.: The National Temple Hill Association, 1969.

Oblinger, Milo M. *Orange County Guide*. Monroe, N.Y.: Orange County Guide, 1956.

"Poughkeepsie According to Platt." *Hudson Valley Magazine*, May 1987. Special insert pp. 4-9.

Price, Willard, and Miller, Wayne. "Henry Hudson's River." *National Geographic*, March 1962, pp. 364-403.

Ringwald, Donald C. *Hudson River Day Line: The Story of a Great American Steamboat Company*. Berkeley, Cal.: Howell North Books, 1965.

Sanderson, Dorothy Hurlbut. *The Delaware & Hudson Canalway: Carrying Coals to Rondout*. Ellenville, N.Y.: The Rondout Valley Publishing Co., 1965.

Shultz, Herbert Lloyd, and Smith, Agnes Scott. *Historic Kingston: 300th Anniversary Booklet*. Kingston, N.Y.: Freeman Publishing Co., 1952.

Twelfth Annual Official Program: Convention and Tournament of the Hudson Valley Volunteer Firemen's Association. Kingston, N.Y.: Hudson Valley Volunteer Firemen's Association, 1901.

Wakefield, Manville B. *Coal Boats to Tidewater: The Story of the Delaware & Hudson Canal*. South Fallsburg, N.Y.: Steingart Associates, 1965.

Wynkoop, F. S.; Chipp, Rodney A.; and Winter, Ann. *The Kingston and Rondout Directory*. New York: William H. Boyd Directory Publishing, 1857.

Index

About the Author

Robert Paul Molay, a native of Chicago, is a 1963 honors graduate of the University of Michigan who went on to earn a master's degree in English from Columbia University as a fellow of the Woodrow Wilson National Foundation. His academic credits also include a year of study at the Sorbonne in Paris, France.

Since 1969 he has resided in the Mid-Hudson Valley, where he became a teacher in the Poughkeepsie public schools and at Oakwood, a Quaker boarding school in Poughkeepsie. In 1978 he joined the effort to save and restore the Bardavon 1869 Opera House in Poughkeepsie.

As a newspaper reporter, feature writer, columnist, and photographer, Mr. Molay gained a wide and loyal readership throughout the Mid-Hudson region. He was associated with Hudson Valley Newspapers in Highland, *The Evening News* of Newburgh, and *News of the Highlands,* Inc., where he was managing editor in 1984-1985. He resides in Goshen, New York and is currently a copy editor at a nationally circulated financial newspaper based in New York City.

He has a daughter, Carrie, and a son, Joshua.

Aerial photographs of lower Broadway and the Newburgh riverfront show the corporate headquarters building of Key Bank as it nears completion. Courtesy of Key Bank